Dancing in the Light

A GUIDE TO AWAKENING

KIM BEAM

Foreword by Isabelle Zimmerman

ISBN: 978-1-966798-85-9

Reviews and Testimonials

"Kim Beam is the REAL DEAL."
~Isabelle Zimmerman, ascension teacher and author
https://www.attractingwisdom.com/
~ Sanjay Raja, Executive Producer
and Host of *Recipe for Wellness* airing on PBS
https://myrecipeforwellness.com/
~ Jen Brown, life coach to teens, young adults, and the parents who
are working so hard to raise them
https://jennbrowncoaching.com/

"Kim Beam is a breath of fresh air and so giving. Helping people find their light…, their directions, and sometimes it's just a word that resonates and gives you clarity."
~ Kelly Bowley, Living Well with Kel
https://livingwellwithkel.com/

"Kim, you're powerful. You're really very, very powerful. And empathetic."
~ Beth Jones, Trauma Mentor, and Best-Selling author of
*Becoming an Empowered Survivor: You, Too,
Can Heal from Trauma and Abuse*
https://empoweredsurvivors.com/

"[Meeting Kim Beam] is really a life-changing experience and I can't say that enough."
~ Brooklyn Calloway, Creator of BrookieLynn's Bungalow
https://www.youtube.com/user/brookielynnsbungalow

Dedication

I dedicate this book to you, my Dear Reader, because you chose to join me in this life adventure. We are in each other's field because you are reading my words and I am sharing your space. You were meant to find me and I was meant to be given a voice in your life. Thank you for allowing me to be words of wisdom and comfort to you. Thank you for creating time and space for us to be together in these pages, in the meditations, and maybe even beyond.

FOREWORD

By Isabelle Zimmerman

Hello, hello, hello!!
Hey... I know we just met.
Is this weird?
This might be weird.
Yup, I already feel ya and love you.

What?! That's crazy talk, right?
How could I already love you?

Well, if you picked up this book, you already love Kim Beam.
And if you love Kim Beam, I love you.
Because I love Kim Beam.

Wait... *I just picked up this book. I don't even really know Kim Beam.*
How could I love her?

Well... here's a little secret: That attraction, that inspiration?
It came from your SOUL.

And your SOUL connected with Kim's SOUL
and my SOUL...
and now we're all in a love FEST.

Silly goose, you didn't just *stumble* on this book.
Magic — the Divine — is sooooo real.
You just haven't been taught to see it and trust it, that's all.

Picking up this book was like a little tap on your shoulder from your SOUL.
A nudge.
A wink.
A Divine message.
A super duper important one.

Here it is:

- It's time to connect with your Spirit Team.
- It's time to remember who you really are.
- This life matters.

You matter.
You are important.

We are in a time of massive transformation — what many of us call The Grand Awakening.
(Don't take my word for it. Google it. ChatGPT it. TikTok it. Whatever and however you research.)

And this book? *Dancing in the Light?*
It's a lifeline.
It's a laugh in the dark.
It's a Spirit Guide in book form — wrapped in Kim Beam's voice:
Part teacher, part best friend, part straight-up channel for Divine wisdom.

Let me tell you another little secret from my own journey.
I've done over 1,000 sessions across 8 years, using hypnosis as a technique for exploring the Soul Field.
(You might think of them as past lives — and that's okay.)

The point is: that's a good data set.
And because I've witnessed so much, over and over again, what I'm about to say is valid and true:

- Your Spirit Team is always talking to you.
- Yes, you absolutely *can* connect with them.
- And connecting means… feeling more LOVE.
- You *can't* mess this up. Seriously.

Kim reminds us of this, over and over again.
She tells the truth.
She shares her stories.

She brings the vulnerability, the awkwardness, the sacred, and the sparkle.

This isn't just a book.
It's an energetic transmission.

So if you're feeling stuck, weird, raw, tired, or just slightly crispy around the edges from life — keep reading.

And I know we just met... but can you promise me one thing?

Don't give up.
Keep an open mind.
Suspend disbelief.

(It's not like I'm asking you to eat worms or something.)

I'm just asking you to move more into *LOVE*.

Judgment is fear, my dear.
It's heavy. It's yucky.

Let me ask you this:
Have you ever felt *good* when someone — or even yourself — judged you?

Okay, okay... *Maybe* if you win a contest and someone judges you the best.
But does it last?
Don't the fearful thoughts creep in anyway?

Self-esteem down the toilet?

So now that we've aired that out — great! You can see it.
Judgment = Fear.

And I'm here asking you to choose...
LOVE.

Why?

Because...

This life matters.
You matter.
And your Team?
They're with you.
Right now.
Reading over your shoulder.
Laughing with us. Crying with us. Cheering you on.

So grab your tea, find a comfy spot, and get ready.
You're not just reading a book.

You're answering the call.
You're dancing in the light.

Let's go.

With big love and tiny sparkles,
Isabelle Zimmerman
Ascension Guide, Spirit Translator, and Fellow Weirdo on the Path.

Table of Contents

Unlock Your Inner Potential:
Free Audio Meditations Gift!

Are you ready to transform your life and connect with your Spiritual Team with clarity and confidence?

Kim Beam has recorded three different meditations to help you connect with your Source. She helps your brain let go and press into the supernatural realms of the higher self and self-discovery.

These meditations were recorded to give you the opportunity to connect with your Spiritual Team in the freedom of your own self-exploration. Feel empowered and confident in the messages you receive from your Source directly, by allowing Kim Beam to help you hear and see what has been there all along - guidance on this path of life and connecting to your Source.

🎁 **What's Included:**

- A Collection of Three Different Guided Meditations: Each meditation is expertly crafted to help you relax, find balance, and connect with your Spiritual Team.

❄️ **Why You Need This:**

- Stress Reduction: Experience profound relaxation and relief from daily stress, helping you to maintain a calm and centered state of mind.
- Emotional Healing: Address and release past traumas and emotional blockages, paving the way for inner peace and personal growth.
- Spiritual Connection: *Deepen your connection with your higher self and intuition, guiding you towards a more fulfilling and purpose-driven life.*

💡 Why This Gift is Essential:

- Convenience: Enjoy these meditations anytime, anywhere, right from your smart phone. Whether you're at home, at work, or on the go, you have instant access to inner calm.
- Expert Guidance: Benefit from Kim's wisdom: she's a qualified Mindfulness Instructor, she has a daily meditation practice, and she has years of training with expert meditators, channelers, and spiritual beings.

  The meditations included are not "Mindfulness Meditations"; they are meant to take you on a journey within yourself with care and expertise.

- **Listen over and over to meet with different members of your Spiritual Team and/or find answers and support to different life questions and struggles as they arise.**
- Free Access: Just click the link below and start your journey to a more peaceful and empowered you!

👢 How to Get Your Free Gift:

Simply go to https://ditl-meditation.kimbeam.com/ to claim your free audio meditations. Start experiencing the benefits today and open the door to a more balanced, centered, and empowered life.

Ready to enhance the journey presented in
Dancing in the Light: A Guide to Awakening?

Scan the QR Code for instant access:

Acknowledgements

To my amazing support team, in no particular order:

Barbra Kogan - Barbra is my "paper" person. Anything stationary, cards for live events, mock book covers, little cards for small notes, she does it all. She sees my wacky requests as lovely challenges and I am so grateful for her support! She runs with my ideas and brings them to life. If you have fancy (or not so fancy) invites to send, personalized stationary you would like to create, create a stamp for your return address on envelopes, or just get creative - she's info@matchpoint stationery.com and https://matchpoint.shop.printswell.com.

Brianna Steimer - I am always so impressed with my Bri-ness. She is professional at all times and remarkable in her resiliency and ability to keep on loving and accepting people for who and where they are. Her story breaks my heart, but at the same time makes me appreciate the strength and fight she has demonstrated over and over again. So, Bri, wherever you wind up, whatever you wind up doing, I know you will do it with all of your passion and heart, because that is how you approach life - open-hearted and aware of the pain this life can bring, while still taking risks and being brave.

Dave Spahl - Dave, I appreciate you so much and your willingness to read, give feedback, and ponder my "wacky" ideas. I know this is foreign for you, and so you stepping into this land and giving me feedback is so helpful. It really helps me know where I need to clarify and support my ideas.

Erin Dolan - Thank you for walking all the journeys with me. From the fundamentalist stick days, to the meditation hours, to the writing of awakening handbooks! Thank you for your unending love through all of it. Your support means everything to me and I appreciate how you are so grounded even when I'm at my most flighty. You are my Erin and I am so grateful for you.

Isabelle Zimmerman - I don't have words for how much Isabelle has had a positive affect on my life. Personally and professionally. She is an ascension teacher and author. Her work has a ripple effect. By healing soul wounds and integrating past life pain, she brings deep healing not only to this lifetime, but to lifetimes past and future. She is the author of the channeled novel, *Unseen Light* and the whole *The Light: The Fae Union Trilogy*. She can be found at https://www.attractingwisdom.com.

John Artinger - John! You never cease to amaze me. All the times you have shown up supporting my endeavors and believing in me. Thank you so much! You really are a truly kindhearted and noble man.

Kelly Bowley - I love that you are my Texas - Alaska friend! I love that you are figuring out your place in the world. Kelly works with individuals who are looking to increase their health and don't just want to be a medical record number. As a former nurse, she brings her professional life together with her personal development around how healing is complete when you combine the soul needs with the body needs. She can be found at https://livingwellwithkel.com.

Michelle Chase - I am so grateful we have come to know and support each other! She received the working manuscript of this book and had it back to me in less than 24 hours. It was impressive, and her feedback was very helpful. She is a woman who gets things done, but also has beautiful insight and a strong intuition. She knows what it means to wait on Spirit and trust for the outcomes you want to see. Michelle can be found at msmichellesigmon@gmail.com. Reach out to her for a tarot reading, a reiki session, or if you just feel like she might have some insight for you!

Rachel Hykel - Rachel's edits on this book pushed me in ways that are so good for this book. Rachel is also my ideal audience, so when she was confused, I knew I needed to add more detail and clarify. She was fabulous in close reading. She was deeply thoughtful about the feedback she gave and why she was giving it. Her reading of the early manuscript helped create a much stronger book for you, Dear Reader. I'm so grateful to her and her time!

Sonya McDonald - Sonya and I filmed our episodes for _Recipe for Wellness_ at the same time. We shared the production house together, along with the filming crew, the director, and the host - Sanjay Raja. It was such a rich time together! Sonya is a board certified transformational life coach and registered nurse with over 30 years experience. She blends her nursing background in a holistic way with her coaching to help clients increase their energy and their peace, and live well despite any challenges or limitations they may face. She has created a 9-pillar of energy intelligence blueprint, which is applicable to any health crisis. Sonya has learned how to thrive and enjoy life while throwing off the symptoms that come with the labels of Rheumatoid Arthritis and Fibromyalgia. She can be found at https://www.sonyamcdonald.com.

Sue Cusumano - Your comments and suggestions on the copy of this book made the book richer. Your thoughts allowed me to see how I was missing the mark slightly in some sections and you really helped me make sure I was being clear and supportive to my reader. Sue is a realtor with Freestyle Real Estate and can be found here: https://freestylere.net/.

The She Rise's Team - You have been so supportive, patient, and thorough in bringing this book to life. Catherine Cruz, Berna De Jesus, Katrina Senne - you have all been so amazing in helping this book come to be! Thank you so much for your dedication, hard work, and time! Hanna Olivas and Adriana Luna - thank you both for your vision and desire to create a platform that creates such amazing opportunities for women to share their dreams, voices, and love!

Introduction

Every time I sat down to write this book, I started with the same introductory words to get myself settled into my Source and Spiritual Team for you:

"In this place, I welcome our highest selves, Source, angels, spirit guides, the superconscious, and any other sources of light (like our heart wisdom) that are working for our highest good.

"I ask the Spiritual Team for wisdom and insight, illuminating dark places, and healing deep wounds.

"We dedicate this time to be centered around our highest good to elevate our vibrations, and bring us into a space wherein we co-create lives we love.

"May this journey, this time, this day, and these moments be a delight, a joy, and absolute Yes! And Huh-zah!"

https://ditl-meditation.kimbeam.com/

I am so thankful that you are here, that you have found your way to this book. I am so thankful that you're letting my words be words of light and direction for your path.

Please know, I know how hard this life can be. I know what the challenges are and I know the kinds of struggles we all encounter. I have stared death in the face and I have walked long roads of healing. I know life might not be easy. I hope these words are a bit of comfort, a bit of direction, and a bit of guidance as you step into your own spiritual awakening.

Please do not wait until Chapter 8 to dive into the meditations I recorded for this book. There is a QR code or the link right there for you to get listening to them now. I want you to get so familiar with them that you don't need them to hear your Spiritual Team. I would love it if you listened to them before going to bed, listened to them on waking up, listened to them in those moments when you have 10 minutes where you think, "I don't know what to do with myself," or you are thinking, "I think I might crawl out of my skin."

Grab one (there are three different ones recorded for you) and listen.

Allow your Spiritual Team the opportunity to speak to you directly.

Their words are more powerful than my words. Your Source's words are more powerful than this little book. If there's anything in this book that can change things, it is the meditations.

The QR code and link are right above. Please use them to listen and be transformed.

This book is channeled, meaning I sat with my Spiritual Team and I gave them permission to use their words for you. I asked them to share, so that you can feel and know them. My Source refers to itself as "We," and they call me, "Kim." I hope these pronouns do not confuse you. My real hope is that their words bring you as much comfort as they bring me.

This life is a journey, a long, meandering path and a very quick blink. Before you know it, time has passed and circumstances that you have been longing for are still not in your life. Please know, I understand being content and being discontent. I understand feeling hope and feeling disappointment. I understand excitement and regret.

I am just as human as anybody else. I might just be a little further down the path of healing, the path of understanding, the path of hearing, the path of contentment, than you might be. This doesn't make me better and doesn't make our roads any less rocky.

I am delighted to be able to support you and share with you. I am excited to reveal my Spiritual Team's truths in real and authentic ways. In ways that I sincerely hope will encourage, lift you up, and help you feel a little less alone.

Awakening can feel really lonely. My sincere desire is for these words to help you feel seen, understood, and appreciated.

My Spiritual Team says this a little later in the book, but it bears mentioning now: As much as you might hate this, the truth is, your Spiritual Team knows what's best for you. I know that's such a challenging thing to hear, because you think you know what's best for you. The more you get to know your Source, the ways your Source talks to you, and the ways your Source comforts you, the easier this life gets. There is less struggle and there is less angst. Please trust me though, learning to hear is a process and one that is talked about regularly in this book – and a reason for the meditations.

In the next chapter, Pre-Words, I discuss both the terms Source and Spiritual Team if these words "tripped you up."

Please feel free to reach out to me with questions, concerns, insights at info@kimbeam.com. I do sincerely want you to know how much I am rooting for your success and happiness.

All my love,

Kim

Pre-Words

This is a conversation I had at the start of my book, *Walk in Courage: Trusting the Whispers of Your Intuition.* These are mainly the same words that opened that book, so forgive me the repetition if you have read them before. However, this is a conversation that is so necessary to get us all on the same "page," if you will indulge me in a pun.

Let's deal with the inherent struggle when talking about anything metaphysical. Let's talk about what I call Source or Spiritual Team. It's the *words* that are the problem – not what it represents. We metaphysical types cannot seem to agree on the word we use.

What is Source when I say it to you, Dear Reader? Is it God? The Universe? Guides? Basic energy? What if someone is tapping into Angels or Stardust? We all use these words interchangeably to mean the same things, and every book I read on the subject has this same discussion in it – what am I going to call that nameless, faceless, beneficent, and compassionate guidance that comes in whenever a person is open to it?

I have spent *a lot* of time thinking about this. So, the next words are true for me. Not necessarily for you.

I like Source because that word is individually defined and doesn't put my opinions, barriers, or limitations on it. You get to create a meaning that is true for yourself when I say, "Source."

So, here's what I ask you to ponder - what do *you* want to call it when I say "Source"?

What is your Source of guidance? Who in the spirit realms do you tap into when you are looking for answers or the information you are craving?

I have a friend who calls it "the Divine" – but I struggle with God and religion. To say I have religious issues would be an understatement, and the word "Divine" smacks of God and organized religion. That doesn't bother her and she embraces Divine as her "Source."

Angels are too limiting – for me, Source is so much bigger than just the Angels.

I have a best friend who calls it, "The Universe." For me, as a term, the Universe feels too big and impartial. However, for her, this term is comforting. It's her definition; it's her "Source."

Guides would be a good term, but sometimes I think my intuition is getting ideas from something bigger than Guides. Also, the idea and belief of Guides is not something everyone is able to subscribe to. (However, I will own, I use the term Guides in the meditations. If this is a struggle for you, change the word in your head to one you like.)

We all have a Source, I think, no matter the name we call it.

I also have found that in my Zoom meetings and at live events, I have been waving my arm in the air in a circular fashion and saying, "My Spiritual Team," which I shorten to "Team."

Whatever it is for you – your higher self, God, Spirit, the Universe – that is what I mean when I say, "Source," or "Spiritual Team," or even just "Team." Even if, for you, Source is just where the nameless, faceless, beneficent, and compassionate guidance comes from, with no other definition than that.

You get to define it. You get to work with it how you will.

It's your Source, after all.

Chapter One

The Script Is *Not* Fully Written

We love you so much and we are thrilled to meet with you here. We have so much to share with you, to tell you, and to help you to know.

Kim has gotten to know us so well. She has taken a deep dive into her history, or rather her soul, and she has come to have a new perspective on life and love in the past six months. We are so excited to be able to join you in the way you see the world, in the way you see how the world turns, and in how you perceive how the world moves, in the way it "books through space" to quote one of Kim's favorite people. It makes sense on one level. You see what you see. What you see is viewed through your eyes and through your perceptions.

We want you to step back and realize that the way you see the world is not the way that other people around you see the world. You know this already. You are aware of this because of the conflicts you get into. You see how things are going. You also see how you think things should go. Then someone steps in and says, "No. No. I see this another way." It's surprising to most humans when they hear of another person's perspective. It's a little shocking when another person's perspective opens the door to new understandings.

Kim often said that she did not want to make decisions based on her own perceptions. Years ago, when she was new in her relationship with us, she knew she had two eyes in the front of her head and they only saw what was in front of her or in her peripherals. She never saw what she called her "six," a term she picked up from watching NCIS. She knew she wouldn't ever see what was behind her and she never knew what she didn't know. So she always thought other people's perceptions, and perspectives, had more value than her own. She always gave other people's viewpoints on situations more merit.

In some ways, she felt it made her weak. That she looked to others. That she didn't trust herself to see it all and know it for what it was. However, she also knew living in a 3D reality, her perception was the only thing she had and she knew that it wasn't rounded out. She knew that there was more. She would go to those people who were in her tight inner circles, and people she trusted very much and say, "Hey, this is what I'm thinking about. What do you think?" Often they would say, "Yeah go for it." Or they would say, "Hey have you thought about this?" and offer another viewpoint. In certain instances, they would say, "Hey, I think you need to protect yourself," or "I think you need to block that person," or "I think that you need to allow that person to not have as much of a voice in your life." Then she would be stumped by their protective statements.

As is true for everyone, you don't know what you don't know. We don't know how else to say that. You *don't* know what you don't know.

We hope to shine a little light on the fact that there are endless possibilities. There are doors. Some of those doors are closed. Some of them are open. The ones that are closed, when you try to open those doors, they may not open right away. Then you assume that the entire thing is not for you. In our reality, it might be that you are not ready yet. Or that door is meant for someone else and another one will open for you.

In this writing we want to explore with you how you find:

Satisfaction,
Delight,
Joy, and
Happiness

in this lifetime, even if what you are seeing is not matching the scenario in your head. It does not mean it is the wrong scenario.

There is so much more here for you and we are so excited to start this conversation with you. We are excited that Kim opened her heart and her gifts to allow us the opportunity to share our thoughts, our dreams, and our desires for you.

This is the bold statement we want you to understand and hear: *The lifetime you are currently living is a play.* You have been given a role and a part and a script. The problem... well, not a problem, but, yes, a "problem" is that you don't know how it ends. The other... well, "problem" is that for many of you, you don't know your purpose for being here in this lifetime.

When actors are handed a script, they are handed the whole thing: the exposition, the rising action, the climax, and the conclusion. They are given the whole story and they know where the story is going, so when they are performing in the opening, they put the right emphasis on lines and looks and gestures to foreshadow the ending. Let us use an example that you might all know from *Harry Potter;* Severus Snape has a role and his role is so important. We as the audience think he is the bad guy, when he may, in totality, be the hero of the entire story. Maybe. But Kim would tell you, he is a very human hero. When she reads *Harry Potter,* as a trained and certified educator, his teaching styles aren't just problematic, they are destructive and abusive. On another level, however, he is playing his role so well.... When the reader gets to Book 7, they realize the whole time the role that he's been playing and how brilliant a light he is. Maybe he was pretending to be such a bad teacher to hide his true role.

In fact, there's a story that in the middle of filming *The Sorcerer's Stone,* J.K. Rowling pulled Alan Rickman, the man who originally played Severus Snape, aside and said, "Here's what you don't know," and she told him the backstory behind Severus. This means, the whole time Alan Rickman was playing the role, Alan Rickman knew Severus Snape's biggest secret and Severus Snape's biggest vulnerability. Alan Rickman knew information the rest of us did not have as he was playing the part. Rickman knew all of the backstory that was still not known to the audience of the movie, and not known to the readers of the book. He had inside intel and that shaped his portraying of Severus Snape.

When you are born, you are not given the script of your lives. There is a reason for this. Part of that reason why you don't know the full outline of what is to come is because your decisions are not yet made and the absolute path is in your hands. You came here for experiences, for opportunities, to feel, and be physical on this earth. There is a purpose and a rough outline. That is all.

If you know too much, you won't play your roles properly. There are things you are to accomplish in this lifetime. There are things set out for you to do. You have tasks at hand to accomplish, roles from previous lifetimes that you need to clean up, explore further, and push into deeper understanding.

This idea of past lives might be a bit controversial for some of you. We understand that it might be hard. We ask that you suspend disbelief at this time. Just roll with the idea, and if that makes you uncomfortable, just recognize it makes you uncomfortable.

There are purposes and things that you are to accomplish in this lifetime. You are placed here at this time, with this cast of characters around you for a reason. There are specific tasks you have set out to accomplish before you got here. The truth is, you may choose not to complete them. You may not do it. It's your choice. You get to say yes or no, ultimately. When the choice point comes, you have the choice to either do it or not.

What if you don't do it? What if you say, "No," to the ultimate purpose of your being here at this time and place with all these people around you?

Well, you will get another opportunity. This is why some of you talk about your repeating patterns. You know that you date the same kinds of people. Or you take the same kinds of jobs. Or you wind up with the same kinds of bosses. There is a lesson for you to learn in these experiences. Until you learn the lessons, you will keep having the same experiences, until you choose differently.

We love you so much and we want you to hear this so clearly.

You can't screw this up. This is something that Kim worries about all the time. When she has broken up with a guy, or takes a new job and leaves her comfort zone, or even when her father died, she felt that she was "f-ing" up her life. That she was making such large mistakes that she wouldn't be able to "come back" from them.

We want you to hear this so clearly. You can't make a mistake. You can't blow it. You can't mess this up - in the big, ultimate grand scheme of things.

Yes, you're given opportunity, after opportunity, after opportunity to figure it out. At the same time, there is nothing but love and support for you as you struggle to find your way. It doesn't matter what job you have. It doesn't matter who you marry, necessarily.

Listening to your gut is the most important thing. Listening to your Team or Source is the most important thing. (Please see Pre-Words in the opening of this book for definitions.)

Everything that occurs is useful.

So even if you go down a road or a path that's really not meant for you, it will still be useful for you on this earth experience, because everything is an opportunity for learning and growth. You are here to learn and grow. That is ultimately why you are here. Your soul wanted the physical experiences that is life on Earth and you came here to expand your understanding of life and love on this planet. So whether you are poor and struggle with housing and utilities and phone bills and just bills in general or whether you're super wealthy and your struggle isn't financial necessarily but something else - you came here with the main purpose to learn how to let your Source be important and for your ego to be less important. Being poor or wealthy doesn't matter. Your Source will use any of your circumstances to get you to where you want to be. All of your experiences become useful. You do have a say in what happens. You get to choose if you're going to go to college or not, and if you go to college, which college you're going to go to.

You are not handed the full script of your life. One, that's for your protection - if you knew everything you would be bored and where's the adventure in that? And two, who you are, and who you are becoming - you will always have choice points along the way. You are co-creating your life. You are creating the reality you see in front of you with your Source, discovering your life purposes, and your choices and preferences along the way.

You get to choose these things.

In the next chapter, we want to talk to you about how you don't really have to worry about anything.

Chapter Two

The Script *Is* Fully Written

This is so important for you to understand.

While some of the experiences and decisions have less importance, at the same point, there are certain things that you are meant to accomplish in this lifetime.

There are relationships you are meant to heal.

There are relationships you are meant to break patterns with.

The relationship with yourself and your Source needs attention and love.

These things are important.

Dear Reader, you have been given opportunities to learn and heal. Over and over.

This lifetime in which you are living and reading these words is an extremely important lifetime.

It might be uncomfortable to hear; however, there are things that you *absolutely* must accomplish in this lifetime. There are things that are non-negotiable. There may be marriages you must create and then divorce from. It may be relationships you start and then stop. Or relationships you choose to faithfully commit to for your entire lives. It may be moments with a truly terrible or maybe a truly wonderful boss. It might be a job that makes your soul soar. It might be going out on your own on an entrepreneurial path, or leaving your country of origin to live as an emigrant in another country. These are the kinds of things that are "musts" in your life.

Some things are just "fated."

Your Source will help you establish the experience to complete those "must be accomplished" tasks.

We want you to hear this so clearly - if you hear nothing else, hear this: *it is not on you to find the experiences.*

The experiences will show up for you. We promise. Just like there is a script of your life of things that are going to happen, it doesn't mean you have to go and make those things happen. It is your Team's responsibility to make the experiences that are "musts" appear on your table before you. Your job is to be present, to be open, and to be willing to learn as you move forward on your path.

One of the hardest things for Kim to learn in this lifetime has been letting go of singleness versus the idea of couplehood. She has always been wondering who the guy is going to be. Kim has always been a little obsessed with dating, who she was crushing on, and when she would find her person. This was a bit of a focus for a long time in her life. The times she was most content about her future and what her path should be was when she was in a committed relationship with someone. It was in these times that she felt she didn't have to worry about any of the details - who, when, and how.... She was able to just be present with the person she had chosen to commit to. Only, those men? They were not men who would have been able to be present with Kim as she transformed, healed, became who Source needed her to become in order to fulfill the purposes of this lifetime. So, out of frustration of how her dating life was going, there were times she signed up with a matchmaker, or was active on dating apps. (Let us say, those dates were dismal failures too - full of frustration and hurtful statements from the men. They were not the kinds of men that would allow Kim to pursue her future and they would have been too controlling.) In other moments, also out of frustration, she swore off dating all altogether. Also, we find it interesting the relationships that meant the most to her were ones that started because she pursued guys who said they weren't interested in dating – she loved the challenge. None of those men fulfilled the desire of her heart, which was to be pursued, wooed, and made a priority.

One of these people Kim was in contact with in her early 20's. He was a couple of years younger, left his well-paying job as a chemist, and decided to bicycle around the continent of South America. While he was biking, Kim would write him emails with prophetic words – and denied having a crush on him. When he said he was interested in dating someone in South America, Kim then wrote him an email about how to discern if this person was "for him," but also said, in essence, "I want you to choose me."

He didn't.

Today, he won't (even if he wanted to) because Kim is not walking in the Christian faith.

But, he will occasionally send her a text that says, "God wants you to come back to him," to which she says while he is out in dangerous places around the globe doing Bible translation, "Keep your sorry ass safe and make sure you come home in one piece or you will have to answer to me. No being all brave hero out there either."

These two entities, Kim and this fellow, have such mutual love and respect for each other, but they will never be together as a couple.

If Kim had known when she was 23 or 24 that she would be single well into her 40s, almost her fifties, she may have lost her temper. She might have given up hope in general. But, we needed her to become involved in a couple of relationships for some key reasons.

Though none of these relationships lasted longer than three years, she has learned much from them.

One of the things that is of note in her relationships is that Kim has been healing soul experiences in her past lives in this lifetime. This has been a lifetime of healing.

Recently, Kim was seeing somebody, very briefly, and it became clear that he wasn't making her a priority. She let him go, because she has had enough of men not making her a priority.

We want to say this of Kim's relationships. The past couple of people she has been in relationship with have been men where the situation felt weighty and complicated. These were individuals that needed pattern healing from previous lifetimes, so they weren't simple relationships. They were soul connection relationships that needed more healing and space in this lifetime. It takes time and a willingness to heal to create something new, something deeper, and something more loving and kind.

The relationships that you have in your life are here for a reason. They are here to teach you something. They're here to heal something and often it is both to heal and to teach. We ask that you don't get down on yourself when you feel you have been repeating patterns, or making what you are judging to be dumb decisions. It doesn't work like that with Source.

We want you to hear that soul growth is the most important thing for us. Your awakening, your quickening to Source is the most important thing to us and so we will use any and everything in our power to get your attention, even if that means situations that you would really never pick for yourself. It is Source's job to create the experiences. It is Source's job to find the people and bring them into your life.

We touched on this in *Walk in Courage: Trusting the Whispers of Your Intuition*, but we want to open it up a little more than we did there. We have more information to share now and it's become such a beautiful "love" story of friendship and mutual regard. To recap for those who may not have read *Walk in Courage* – Kim saw a man in a coffee shop. When she noticed him and how adorable he was, she heard someone call his name. Ironically, in that moment, in that same coffee shop, Kim was downstairs and the man upstairs was her college professor. Kim had a crush on that college professor sitting upstairs. When the cute man in front of her had the same name as the professor upstairs, she decided it was just too many people with that name. Though Kim was drawn to the man in front of her, with his cute socks, gangly limbs, and goatee, she decided to let him go.

Kim thought, "I can't be crushing on two 'Ruperts' at the same time," to make up a name.

Three years later, Kim was walking down the hallway at her new-ish job at a local hospital. She saw this tall man, with a beard, and gangly limbs walking toward her. She saw him and decided to just keep walking, act like she didn't notice just how adorable he was. Instead, he called over to her. "Hi! How are you doing?"

Kim thought, "Oh my gosh, who is this guy?" As they stood in the hallway and spoke to each other for over 45 minutes, she thought, "I am in trouble."

Ultimately, they became really good friends. However, the friendship transpired, and however intense or overwhelming their experiences together were, in the end this friendship became a source of healing for both of them. It is a source of mutual respect, love, acceptance, hope, and peace.

The whole story is not something Kim could have orchestrated herself. She could not see him in a coffee shop, let him go, and then see him three years later in her place of employ. She couldn't have made that happen. Kim could not have created the coffee shop moment and she couldn't have created the meeting in a hallway. There is no way she could have created his importance.

More than that, she couldn't fabricate the healing that his presence would be in this lifetime.

This relationship is probably the most powerful dating relationship in her life so far. She stepped up and stepped into the energy of angst, and overwhelm over and over again in this relationship. Then, with soul work, she transformed that negative energy and transmuted it into mutual respect, kindness, regard, and acceptance. She could not do this on her own. She needed her Source to help create all of these experiences and all of these opportunities. If she had done this on her own, she absolutely would have mucked it up.

We created this opportunity for her.

We did this for her. We helped her walk this out. From the days she spent weeping, to the days she worked to forget him, to the day when she reached out to him in peace and reconciliation, to their mutual agreement they wanted to stay in touch with each other, but they had to work out how that was going to happen practically.

There are things that you cannot do without your Team. Being open, receptive, and willing to hear and listen is what creates difference, change, opportunity, and healing.

The people in your life right now are here for a reason.

The people who are coming into your life are coming into your life for a reason. You may not understand that reason right now. You might think that these people are hurtful or mean, or you may think they are wonderful and delightful. Whatever the reason they are here, you did not bring them in.

Let us pause here for a moment to clarify that you did have *some* say in bringing them in. You brought them in through your vibration and the choice to act or not. At the same point, you, *personally*, did not create the circumstances which brought them into your life.

You may have gone online, bumped into their profile, and now they're in your life, right? But you found their profile because Source brought their profile to you. They could have been on a different platform; you could have been on a different platform; or you might not have been on a platform at all.

Everybody has a story about how they met their person (or lost their person). Everybody has a story and in their story there is a bit of Wonder and Magic as to how that happened.

The people in your life are there for a reason. That reason is a soul reason and is incredibly important. Source does not just leave that to chance, but they take that over and make sure that you interact with the people you are supposed to interact with in this lifetime. They make sure that you have the experiences with the people you are supposed to. You do not have to go out and manufacture or create these experiences. In most instances, you don't even know that you are supposed to be having these experiences. It's not your job to make this happen. It's your Source's job.

We don't want you to worry. We don't want you fretting about your life. Some of the major experiences are for your Source to settle. Yes, there is work for you to do, and we will get to that. For the most part, for the experiences you are meant to have, you cannot manufacture the circumstances of those occurrences. All you can do is create the right atmosphere for magic to happen. We will talk about how you do that in the next chapter.

Chapter Three

Your Role in Creating a Life You Love

As Kim is typing this, she is currently sitting at the beach, on a back porch with the ocean waves in her ears.

She could be reading a book right now.
She could be meditating.
She could be exercising.
She could be making dinner.
She could be sleeping.
She could be going for a walk on the beach.
She could be texting a bloke (though there isn't a bloke to text at the moment).
She could be doing a lot of other things.

Instead she's sitting with us, for you.

She's listening to us, for you, to help you create lives you love.

The thing is and this is so important we hope you hear this clearly. (We love you so much.) **You are also responsible for helping us create a life you love**.

There is an expression inside of Buddhist philosophy that is, "Chop wood; carry water."

"Chop wood; carry water" means that while you are in your meditation sit, and while you're trying to be spiritual, and while you're trying to create a spiritual life by meditating, there is also daily work that needs to be done. It's a balance between the meditation sit and the work of daily life.

There's also an applicable expression inside of Christianity that says a person is "So spiritually minded, they are no earthly good."

We each have work to do that is assigned to each of us as our "job," or "purpose," or "mission," in this lifetime.

The writing of this book doesn't happen without time, space, energy, typing, being present with what's present, and allowing the words to come out. These things need to happen. You need human hands and arms in order to create the spiritual world you are looking to create in this lifetime. If you want to see difference in your life, if you want your life to be different, if you want opportunities to be different, if you want to see growth, change, and positivity flourish inside your life, then there is work you need to do in order to create that atmosphere and to create those outcomes. You can't sit in a dark room all the time and lament the fact that you don't have what you want. There is a part we all play to create. Source has its part; you have your part too.

Source asks, "Well, what have you done to create the life you love?"

We know it seems backwards from the last chapter where we said Source will do it, and now we're saying you have things to do too. The truth is, if you aren't willing to get up and move and, like Kim, be in a coffee shop or walk down a hallway, then we can't have opportunities land for you. We need you to be doing a little bit of the work yourself. It's not all just going to land in your lap.

In her book *Walk in Courage: Trusting the Whispers of Your Intuition*, you need to be working on your vibration.

You need to be working on your baseline levels of emotion.

You need to be learning how to hear us and trusting us to know what it is you are looking to create in this world.

There is some movement you need to create by doing your daily routines. If you're looking for a miracle, you need to not just be in your house wishing for a miracle. You need to be going to the grocery store, going to work, and stepping up.

If you have a disability, we understand that there are different circumstances, but there is still a part for you to play.

Overall, there is a need for all of us, not just those who are limited, to not give up, and not just accept some circumstances as being limiting....

Being in joy, being in passion, and being excited for other people is a way to create better experiences. The more excited and joyful you are, the more opportunity there is for you to change your circumstances and create a life you love.

There is work for you to do and that work could be work for yourself, such as knitting a sweater or writing a journal, or it could be work for somebody else where you intentionally volunteer with somebody who is now housebound or you start writing a book that you think is going to support millions of people.

You have work to do.

There are tasks given to you specifically to complete. Some of those tasks could be spiritual tests to find out if you are ready to take on the next level of responsibility and spiritual growth. Other tasks for you to complete are:

- How much are you loving yourself and how well do you show it outwardly?
- How much do you appreciate others and how well do you show that appreciation outwardly?
- How much do you speak your own truth, even if you know it could hurt someone else?

These are not necessarily easy to answer questions because sometimes taking a hard look at yourself isn't always comfortable.

The idea that some of the experiences in front of you are of your own making is also not comfortable.

We have things we would like you to accomplish. There are roles and tasks that are a part of your purpose – so let's get into the nitty and the gritty about your purpose in this lifetime. If you're going to dance in the light, you need to know that one, you're in the light and two, that what you're doing lights you up.

Everybody is born with a reason for being here.

Take a look at yourself for a moment.

- Look at the work you currently do – what parts of that work excite you?
- What things light you up?
- What stories did you tell yourself about your future when you were little?
- What were your dreams when you were small, before people told you, and before you told yourself, you couldn't have those dreams?

Let's explore that last one just a little bit more.

It might not feel like it, but those childhood dreams are maps to helping you find your soul purpose in this lifetime. They shine light onto your soul's intention of learning and growing. We don't need to get into the circumstances of why those dreams changed or why they died. We don't need to talk about the specific stories of that pain or disappointment.

(If you are living your childhood dream, are you sure? Really sure? Kim thought she was living a childhood dream of being a teacher when she became a teacher - only that wasn't the original dream. The original dream was to be a writer and speaker. Then she wanted to be a marine biologist. Then she wanted to be a teacher. Go back to the *original* dream.

If you are sure you are living your dream, read on and know that some of this is asking you to make sure that you are fully alive. Everyone, even Kim, needs to check her light and make sure what she is doing is really on purpose.)

What we do need to talk about it is how to light the fire of your passion.

Because there is work for you to do.

Work that is meaningful and alive and is created specifically for you.

There are some people who are really, really good at their jobs. They're just amazing at the work they do. Almost like they were created to fill the role of the position they are holding.

Kim knew a man at the hospital who was tasked with the job of raising 25 million dollars in his development role. He and his business team raised 27 million. He was then offered a new job with a new assignment. In the new assignment, he was tasked with the role of raising 60 million in 6 years and he raised 67 million in 3 years. He is really good at his job. One could make the case that he is exactly in the role that he is supposed to be in. One could make the case that he is fulfilling his purpose in this lifetime. He is flourishing by creating avenues of revenue for nonprofits.

It's remarkable when you bump into somebody who is doing exactly what they're supposed to do. They are in the zone and the sweet spot of their purpose. You see it because there is evidence of it. They seem magical. They seem like what they do is easy, even though it's near impossible.

The gymnast, Simone Biles, is a person that comes to mind as somebody who makes things look really easy, but in reality she is an almost impossible to beat gymnast. She has created new and sometimes almost illegal vaults. She had a rope climbing competition with her now husband (who might have been her fiance at the time), and she beat him to the top, which is all upper body strength. She does miraculous things with her body, but she makes it look easy. This is possible because she is in the sweet spot of her purpose.

When you are in the sweet spot of your purpose, there's nothing you can't do. What you do looks impossible and other people around you ask, "How did you accomplish that?" When you are really in your sweet spot, you just shrug your shoulders and there isn't much of an answer other than, "It's what I do."

However, when you are not in your sweet spot, you are actually fighting yourself and it's harder to get anything done. If you're doing things that aren't a part of your soul purpose for being here, the work you do, whether it's professional or in your own house or in your other spheres of being, it will be challenging. It doesn't come naturally or easily. People watch you and think, "There are easier ways to do this." Sometimes you get coaching on how to do what you are attempting to do better, more efficiently. The truth is, often this coaching is insulting and just reminds you, "You are not in your soul purpose."

Kim feels she spends way too much time in her kitchen. Part of that is because Kim does spend way too much time in her kitchen. Kim now eats gluten-free, dairy-free, and sugar-free. She doesn't eat processed food. Because she doesn't eat processed food, everything has to be cooked in her kitchen, which takes up a lot of time.

She's not completely happy with that. It's not her zone of genius and she feels there are other things she would rather be doing. She multitasks and uses that time in the kitchen somewhat wisely in that she listens to romance novels and books on audio at something like 1.75 to 1.85 speed. She devours literature, as she spends hours and hours in her kitchen. She says if she could she would hire a personal chef and give someone else the opportunity to cook for her. Someone who really loves to spend that time in a kitchen. Kim would rather be speaking at her live events, hosting people on her podcast, being in her intuition to help others find hope and healing. These are things that are sweet spots for Kim.

One could even make the case that Kim is in her sweet spot when she's working at the hospital and she is able to help families maneuver a challenging discharge, or when there's a challenging case to get out of the hospital. Kim is somebody who can make a miracle happen and establish a safe discharge inside of what appears to be particularly challenging circumstances.

However, hear this. Just because Kim is good at hospital work, it's not inherently her purpose. It was a mode to help her grow and be ready for the experiences that come next. We allowed her to have "sweet spot" moments because it was a growth space. It is not her "purpose" space.

For you, though, how do you find your sweet spot? How do you find the things that make you lit up and excited?

Let us ask you again - what were the dreams you had when you were little? What were you going to be and do when you believed all of the resources and all of the opportunities would open for you?

Or better yet, what was the job that the moment you heard it was a job, or a "thing," and you thought, "That. I want that."

For Simone Biles, we are positive she started at an extremely young age and gymnastics was always a thing for her. Same with Taylor Swift – music was in her life at a very young age.

Do you know the fashion designer, Max Alexander? He has shown his fashions at New York's Fashion Week. He also now has a goal to be a designer for the dresses at the Met Gala. He is seven years old and considers some of the biggest names in fashion design his friends.

He told his mother at age four he wanted to make dresses and his mother supported his dreams.

When Kim was little, she dreamed of becoming a marine biologist. But she also wanted to be a writer and public speaker. She was always telling stories to herself or writing them out. Marine biology died in her sophomore year with Mr. Tietsma. Kim realized while in his class she wasn't in her zone of genius, or rather, his teaching style wasn't her zone of genius. She realized how hard she had to work for a C in his class and how easy it was for her to get an A in English. She realized her dream of being a marine biologist would put her in maths and sciences; she also knew her mind did not find those subjects to be the ease that was English. She took four English classes her senior year, earning an A in all of them, and almost failed physics.

One of Kim's best friends has a daughter. This young woman has overcome her ADHD and inability to focus using a number of coping strategies. She is now medication free, and maintaining straight As in college. She graduated high school with a dual diploma, both a high school diploma and an associates degree from her local community college. She is an avid figure skater, a passion and talent she learned she possessed at the age of two or three. She also has found in her course of studies that she adores spreadsheets and her love of spreadsheets has helped others keep organized. This young woman, as a Sophomore in college, has been hired by a CEO of a major figure skating organization in the United States and has been invited to major figure skating events to help the CEO and other directors stay organized. Her spreadsheets are that good. She has found a way to have a job in college, doing what she loves, in an organization that has a purpose she believes in. They have asked her and have given her more and more responsibility because everything about this position is her passion.

Sometimes, when you are little you don't know what you want. Sometimes, you don't know what will light you up. Sometimes you fall into the position, into the experience, into the circumstances. We want to say that is not a coincidence. When you aren't certain where you are to go, what you are to do, your Source will put you in circumstances and situations that will introduce you to what lights you up and excites you.

Dear Reader, will you pause for a moment and think about what brings you joy, excitement, and delight? What are the moments in your life where you feel like you were in your sweet spot – that you are doing exactly what you are meant to do?

If you haven't found that feeling yet, what is something that pops in your head as we're talking about this that makes you feel like you are alive and hopeful?

It could be a hobby like surfing or paddleboarding. It could also be something organizational or taking long walks in the woods. Or for my best friend's daughter, you know that your spreadsheets put everyone else's spreadsheets to shame.

The point we want to make here is that it doesn't have to be lucrative to be important and light you up. So many people think the thing they adore cannot be the passion they pursue because there may not be money in it initially. The human thinks, "How can I make money doing this?" Like cornhole or pickleball. But if you stick with what you love, you have no idea what doors will open.

On the other side, why does it need to be lucrative to be important? If you enjoy it and it lights you up, that should be enough.

You have no idea where it will lead.

Earlier in this chapter, we posited you with this question: How do you know that you are in the light?

You are in the light when....

- ... you are intentionally seeking peace, intentionally seeking connection, and intentionally seeking calm.
- ... you are looking for your intuition and your Source knowledge to be greater than the information you have in your head.
- ... you decrease the importance of the reality of this world.
- ... you realize that there is something bigger going on and you are willing to let that something bigger be bigger than you are.
- ... you have knowledge that drops into your head or your heart and you act on it.
- ... you trust your heart-knowledge and know it to be reliable and true.
- ... you choose that you are going to be in the light.
- ... you choose an energy vibration that is higher than the energy vibration you hang out at all the time and you press into higher and higher energy vibrations.
- ... you allow the light to guide you.
- ... you integrate knowledge of yourself, the world, and those around you in ways that are more loving, kind, compassionate, and understanding.

Once you are in the light, it is easier to find your purpose. Once you are in the light, it is easier to know that what you are doing is the thing that lights you up. Once you are in the light, you can feel and see how you have been guided to those experiences that lead to your happiness.

There is work for you to do. There's the choice to be in the light and then there is the choice to find the sweet spot in your life.

Source creates the perfect circumstances for chance meetings and opportunities and the experiences they want you to have. You also have a part to play.

If you are supposed to write a book, you need to pick up the pen. If you're supposed to be a famous soccer player, you need to be passionate about soccer – playing, practicing, and watching. If you're supposed to be a famous gymnast, you get yourself into spaces with the right coach in the right place at the right time.

This makes us think of Taylor Swift and how she used to live in Pennsylvania. However, she knew what she wanted for her life. She convinced her family to move to Nashville so she could have more opportunities in the music industry. Every member of Taylor Swift's family had to be in the light in order to agree to pick up their entire lives and move to support her dreams. Taylor Swift's whole family had to see and believe in her true purpose. This is why it's so important that the people around you are the right people around you.

We want to talk more about this in the next chapter.

Just as much as it's important to know who you are and what lights you up, it is so important *who* you surround yourself with. *Who* you surround yourself with matters more than you know. The people around you have the power to lift you up, bring you into deeper levels of your purpose, bring you into even more light and love. Or they have the exact opposite effect and cut you down. We are so excited to talk to you about this in the next chapter.

Chapter Four

Your Great Cloud of Witnesses

The people you surround yourself with are extremely important.

As you step into the light and make choices to be in the light, you may find that the people you have surrounded yourself with may no longer feel like a good fit.

This can be so challenging. When some people choose the light and pursue its growth, often they are surrounded by people they have known for a long time. Sometimes, they are surrounded by their big and intrusive families. Or they could be surrounded by their close circle of friends brought even closer by years of shared experiences.

Stepping into the light changes you. When that happens, you may find the people who you have been calling your friends may not feel the same anymore. You may not feel like you belong or are understood. Perhaps, you no longer resonate with them.

You may find yourself annoyed, bothered, bored, and/or irritated. You may find yourself asking, "How many times am I going to have this same conversation?"

You may find yourself asking, "Where are my people?" or "Why are these people not my people?"

You may find yourself deciding that it is better to be alone and may choose to be a bit lonely rather than hang out with people who pull you down.

When you step into the light, you change your vibration – you raise it up. When you raise your vibration, you positively impact your experiences. You will find that what you find important and what matters to you will also shift. You will come to realize what you are looking for in this lifetime is going to be different as well. You may find that what you value and want to talk about will also shift.

The light shines into your dark spaces and transmutes them. You are changed and shifted as a result.

Before stepping into the light you were content with whatever, and when you let the light in, it shines on all of your lifestyle choices and makes some of those choices uncomfortable. You might find that you no longer want to indulge in snack foods, or drinking, or partying. You might find that you are no longer able to watch horror movies like you did, or read scary books. You might find that something like playing soccer or acting, which had been a passion, is no longer a passion.

This is confusing enough. Things you loved, you no longer love. Or people you really felt connected to, you no longer feel connected to.

When you step into the light something shifts. That change is an internal shift. Once that switch happens, you are no longer the same. What was exciting to you before will no longer be exciting and what is exciting to you now will be unusual for you. You might feel a little like you are losing your mind. You might feel like you're a weirdo. You will feel a little like there is something wrong with you.

We're going to share a story about Kim that's a little vulnerable for her. She never really had close friendships. She didn't feel understood, until her best friend from high school, Carolyn. (For those of you who don't know, Carolyn was diagnosed with a brain tumor nine months before Kim was diagnosed with Hodgkin's Lymphoma. She fought hard and loved harder. In November 2018, she reluctantly left, no longer able to withstand the onslaught of the cancer.) Then in college, she made friends with people she really connected with, only they were seniors when she was a freshman. They all graduated and it took her a long time to find people she connected with, again. In some ways, if we are honest, she never really felt like she connected with anyone in college like she did with the ones who graduated her freshman year.

Even with her friends in college, she felt like she was on the outside. She felt like a bit of an oddball. Post college she kept in touch with some people that she resonated with over the years. There are other friendships that Kim takes responsibility for how those friendships ended. We, as her Team, would like to add that those friends didn't do the work to make things better either. She made friends at new churches. The funny thing about these church friends? Many of them were significantly older than Kim. Kim was hanging out with 60-year-olds when she was in her late 20s and early 30s.

The people Kim resonated with were people who had more maturity and wisdom. She didn't want to be out partying. When she got together with people who were more her age, and also in the church, she found that she didn't have a lot to say to them. They didn't have a lot to say that Kim connected with either.

When she decided it was time to leave the church and no longer follow the teachings of religion, the friends from the church fell away. Instead of supporting and being curious about her new understanding of the world, they kept trying to insist she "come back to Christ." Instead of relationships that were built on mutual love and support, she no longer felt understood. She didn't feel heard and she didn't feel supported.

Another issue was Kim had close friendships with guys. Their significant others had problems with those friendships. Kim worked with a man with whom she joked that they shared a brain, because they understood each other so well. This friend really pushed Kim in ways she now values. He was a Buddhist and a vegetarian. He saw the world so differently from Kim's Christian perspective that he helped her grow. Ultimately, the strain of his wife's needs and the closeness of the friendship caused the friendship to end.

Now that she's out on her own, no longer involved in a religious community, she doesn't know how to make friends. She bumps into people. She sees them. She hangs out with them a little. But it's hard to make that stick.

Kim doesn't have people that she hangs out with because so many people are wrapped up in their own lives and Kim doesn't feel like she lives in a space where she can invite people over. So, Kim doesn't have community the way she would like community.

Also the people she would want community with are not so easy to find. Kim doesn't drink. She doesn't party. There are many things Kim doesn't do that other people do, and so she feels isolated. This adds to her feeling like she's not like everyone else.

Her closest friends live so far from her. Kim now lives outside of Philadelphia in Pennsylvania. Her best friend from college, the one who graduated at the end of her freshman year, currently lives in Abu Dhabi. Her best friend from her first year of teaching lives outside of Newburyport in Massachusetts. She's made a couple of good friends who live down in Florida. One of her good friends from her first graduate degree lives in Richmond, Virginia. She just made a friend she is so so grateful for – who originally lived in Texas and now lives in Kodiak, Alaska. Kim recently made a new connection who lives in South Carolina and Kim knows this is one of her life-long friends.

So, Kim spends most of her time connecting on the phone with these people. They are not in her daily "Let's hang out and go to a movie," "Let's go watch the Super Bowl together," or "Let's, you know, hang out in our backyards together and just be with each other 'cause we enjoy each other".... She doesn't have those kinds of friends. ...and to be honest Kim is really longing for that.

We also want to say that some friendships just aren't meant to go all the way through a lifetime. Some friendships aren't necessarily lifetime friendships. They might be friends for the circumstances you're in and you really resonate in that moment. But, when those circumstances are no longer the same, you no longer really connect anymore. Kim is somebody who loves passionately and so she doesn't let go easily when she finds somebody that she adores. There have been some friendships that were created in schools when she was teaching, besides the ones we've already talked about, that when they ended, she was deeply hurt and even felt a little betrayed.

Recently, she's been repeating a line from a book called *The Hating Game* by Sally Thorne. The main character has her archnemesis in her house because she came down sick at a work event and he helped her get home. She thinks, *"I'm alone in this world,"* to which her archnemesis replies, "Alone in this world? So dramatic."

The more you step into and pursue the light, you will be pushed to pursue transformation, growth, and change. You'll be lit up by the idea of something better. You'll be lit up by the idea of being in your purpose. At that time, you might feel like you're doing things like nobody else does them. That you are alone in these things.

Kim has felt lonely regularly. She now eats in ways that she thinks are "weird." She gets into her unhelpful patterns of thinking and believes something is wrong with her because she can't eat gluten. She can't eat dairy. She can't eat American white refined sugar because she has found three days after the sugar, she is having panic attacks and these massive weeping scenes, sometimes on sidewalks outside of buildings. Because she compares herself to others and says she doesn't eat like everyone else, she thinks there's something wrong with her. We want to say, in reality, this eating super healthy allows her the opportunity to keep her system clean. Her body is her vessel and she's keeping her vessel clean. Because her body is clean, she's also keeping her connection to us clean. She only has this one body to get through this lifetime. Soul and body are connected. By keeping connected to her body, she is keeping her connection to herself, her inner peace, and her inner knowledge clear as well.

We already mentioned Kim doesn't have a ton of friends where she lives. She doesn't have community in the sense that she can call up friends, then they come over, and she hangs out with them. She spends a lot of time alone and this adds to her feeling of disconnection. Her lessons are the beliefs that she is too much, not enough, and there's something wrong with her. If she lets this reality of a lack of close friendships with people who live near her be defining for her, she can really struggle with self-worth, self-acceptance, and peace.

In the Bible in Hebrews 12:1 it says, "Therefore, since we are surrounded by such a great cloud of witnesses, let us throw off everything that hinders and the sin that so easily entangles and let us run with perseverance the race marked out for us."

We don't want to get into the phrase, "the sin that so easily entangles" part. This is a section of religion that really bothers Kim and we don't really want to get deep in those weeds. However what we want to focus on instead is in Christianity there is the belief that you are being lifted up by the people who've gone before you and the people who are around you. The people who are around you are encouraging you. That encouragement enables you to spur yourself on to Greater Heights of faith. Because of those around you, you are able to step up and out and do big, good work.

Your faith stands behind you when you step into the light.

When you step into the light, you are stepping into your Source and Spirit. You are stepping into your truth. You are stepping into your strength. You are stepping into love and we know love to be the most powerful of all emotions. ...that's not the right word though. We know love to be the most powerful solution for any problem. Love brings in connection. Love brings in compassion. It brings in empathy. It brings in joy. Love brings in peace. It brings in reconciliation. The more you love yourself and the more you love others, the more you will be able to create that community of your own personal great cloud of witnesses.

If you are feeling alone or you're feeling like Lucy in *The Hating Game*, where she says, "*I'm alone in this world,*" there are ways to create a community that is in the light. We encourage you to step into your love, your passion, and your excitement. This will help you create the vibration of hope and love. It will raise your vibration and help you attract the kinds of people you are looking for.

We also want to say that when you step into the light and you make the choice to listen to Source, you are choosing your inner strength. There may be some other unintended consequences if this is the first time you have handed yourself and your trust to your Source. There will be some lifestyle changes Source will ask of you to help align you better to Source and to yourself.

Here is the thing. If you are hanging around with people who don't fit, or no longer fit, or if you are looking to make big changes – yes, something new is exciting, but there is a loss here and we don't want to belittle that at all. The loss is sometimes significant.

Your Great Cloud of Witnesses has to reflect who you are and where you are going. Sometimes Source will take people away (as has happened for Kim) for your greater good. There are some things you have to go through alone. Spiritual growth is transformation you travel alone, for the most part - like a caterpillar liquifying and reemerging from the chrysalis as a butterfly.

When you turn to Source and say, "Yes," things shift and change. Some of those things might not be comfortable. You may experience a lack of sleep, a lack of appetite, or even, in some situations, moments of overeating. Aches and pains are all a part of the growth process. The growth process will sometimes affect you physically, not just emotionally and spiritually. We just want you to be aware that when you choose the light, everything gets an upgrade. That upgrade affects your body as well as your psyche, your friendships, your normal way of being in the world, and what you will and will not tolerate anymore.

We encourage you to choose your great cloud of witnesses wisely because they are the people who will either encourage you to do great things or belittle you in order to get you to sit on the couch next to them, eat the chips, watch the TV, and go back to sleep. People don't like it when you get up, start to move, and do things differently. It shines a light on them and on their own shadow. The important thing to remember here is that this has nothing to do with you and everything to do with them. You will find that you are no longer able to do the things you used to do, because the circumstances and the situations are no longer compatible and no longer resonate inside your soul. You will be asking for more and because you are asking for more, you will be creating more. You will need to let go of the old and you need to let go of what no longer serves you. You in your humanness will find this very uncomfortable and challenging. Kim has known people who had to get divorced, who had to change jobs, who had to move across the country, and who had to face their own inner demons.

These changes were two fold: it was supportive to the growth they were looking to bring into their lives and it allowed them to create space for the right people to come into their lives. They were looking for people who would support them as they endeavor new, big, and exciting things.

That is exactly what you are looking for. You are looking to find ways to support the growth you want to occur in your life. You are also looking for people who see the vision you have for your life and spur you on in the greatness you want to build. They will be excited to stand behind you and cheer you on as you run marathons to create a life you love.

Sometimes, when you are looking to bring in something, something else has to be let go of. In the next chapter, we want to explore how to handle the discomfort and pain of loss.

Chapter Five

How to Handle the Pain of Loss or Change

Things happen that are extremely painful, like being fired from a job, or a sudden and harsh break up, or a fire. These things are devastating losses. How you react to them truly matters. You have choice points all along the way and we don't want to belittle the pain that comes from sudden loss. That pain matters and we want to hold space for that pain. At the same time, we also want to point out that when something happens that is out of your control and seems negative, there is something bigger at play. Instead of jumping from one circumstance to another circumstance quickly, we ask that you pause, listen, and seek higher truth, which we will explore in this chapter.

Often when something challenging happens, you pull into yourself or go about your patterns in specific ways so that you don't feel. This reaction is not a "bad" reaction; it's just your normal coping mechanism. It's your way of protecting yourself from the pain. You are dealing with it in a way that works for you. Some people like to exercise. Some people like to drown themselves in their work. Some people find other ways of running away.

We would like to challenge you to not run away.

Pain. Loss. Hurt. These have a significant place in the growth cycle.

There will come a time on the planet Earth when you won't need pain and loss in order to create growth. There are some in humanity now who have this quality – they embrace growth for growth's sake. There will come a time when humanity will embrace growth for growth's sake and not hesitate to change. They will move through growth with ease. Where humans will be excited to grow just to have the experience of growing. There will come a time when, collectively, humanity will be excited to change just to transform.

However, right now in the 3D reality, the paradigm is stuck so that you, as humanity, for the most part, don't change unless there's a catalyst or a force to change. It takes a loss. It takes pain. It takes being so uncomfortable with where you are that you look around and you go, "Okay I'm going to do something different."

The truth is what you do when you are in pain and what you do when you've had a loss really does matter. Instead of following your normal patterns after a loss or after you experience something that causes grief, we would like to challenge your normal coping strategies.

We would like you to take a moment. Please stop and think about a previous pain moment experienced. How did you respond? Did you attempt to run away emotionally? Or maybe you tried to run away physically? Did you bury yourself at work? Did you find friends and social events and drown the pain in noise and movement? Did you drink or use a substance to make it go away? Did you get into reckless or dangerous activities? Did you sign up to go sky diving?

Kim's father died in November 2019. When she was managing his memorial service and coping with the woman formerly known as her step-mother, Kim said, "When this is all over, I'm going to Nepal on a four week silent retreat." Kim knew her emotions were raw and she needed time to just be with the loss and pain. For the record, that memorial service never happened - the Pandemic cancelled it and she did get five weeks of mostly silence at the Himalayan Institute in the summer of 2022. But Kim also took the time of the 2020 Pandemic to meditate for an hour a day, be authentic with herself, and she worked with the Superconscious to learn to overcome her pain.

In another example, Kim fell in love with a man who "set her free," by breaking up with her. But Kim didn't want to be set free. She wanted a life with him. That loss caused her heart to break open. She cried. A lot. Instead of going, going, going, and doing, doing, doing, she put herself on her meditation cushion. She allowed herself to feel the pain of it. She allowed the tears to flow. For months, months, and months, she allowed the tears, but then she got sick of the tears. She went to see a hypnotherapist and told the hypnotherapist, "I need to stop crying." Working with the hypnotherapist got the tears to stop in one session, but that didn't stop the internal pain. Kim sat with that internal pain for a really long time. She allowed it to be there and she allowed it to change her.

Did you hear that last line? She allowed the pain to transform her. She didn't squash it or force healing. She allowed it time and space and breath. In time, that "allowing" created transformation.

Many societies on Earth have decided tears are a sign of weakness. They have decided that tears, a show of emotion, are unprofessional and undignified. However, we fully know that tears are a release of emotion. They are movement. We want you to know that tears are not painful. Tears are actually a release. Tears are freedom from the prison of pent up emotions. Tears are letting emotions out of the body rather than imprisoning them inside. Blocking tears traps old emotions in your body that could have moved out long ago if you allowed yourself to cry.

Tears are also a lubricant that helps heal a broken heart. Kim works in a hospital and met a man recently who was scheduled to be brought down to the Cath Lab to have heart surgery just minutes after Kim met with him. In that meeting with Kim, this patient said that his son had recently died and he was struggling to grieve. He wasn't allowing the emotional rollercoaster to run its course. He said that when his son died, his heart broke. He said this physical heart surgery was because his son emotionally broke his heart. He said he wasn't able to allow the grief to move freely in his body and it messed up his physical heart. He knew it to be true inside his body.

Healing really matters.

Taking time to recognize the pain and the loss is not wasted time. It is not selfish. It is not slacking off.

The way grief happens in the body is different for everybody and what one person's body needs is going to be different from what another person's body might need. What one person needs to heal is going to be different from what another person needs to heal. However, when you are in grief, certain facts are true.

You need more sleep. You need more time in quiet. No loud noises, no extreme voices. You almost need a decompression chamber – a bathtub, a salt float bath at one of those fancy spa places, an opportunity to put your head in water will really change how you feel about your circumstances.

When Kim was struggling with letting that man who broke her heart go, she put herself in a soak and float which is a two foot pool filled with salt water so dense it's like the Dead Sea. The amount of salt in the water forces you to float.

As Kim floated around this shallow pool in a little enclosed room with a glowing blue light in the pool, she had the thought that she didn't want to live her life without him being in her life. This thought settled in her body, but then her very next thought was, "But I'm doing that. I'm living without him." She paused on that and realized she was doing okay. She was okay and he wasn't in her life. She would not have had that realization if she had not given herself the quiet and the space. We would also say water is a conduit to Spirit and if you can get in water, it will help you heal.

For you? We will say it is okay to *want* to run away from your emotions. It is okay to *want* to not feel.

However, we will not stop there.

We will boldly say, because we love you so much, it is not okay to run away from your emotions. It is not okay to run away from how you feel.

This is so important, we want to rephrase this so that it can be positively stated. Positive statements have a bigger impact and a more lasting effect. So we need you to hear this in the best way possible:

You need to feel your emotions. You need to be in touch with how you are reacting in any circumstance.

If you cut off your emotions because they are too painful, you are cutting off *all* of your emotions. You can't just cut off the negative ones. When you cut off your feelings because you don't want a negative emotion, you cut off all of your feelings. Even the good ones. You can't cherry pick the emotions you want and the emotions you don't want. Your emotions are either on or off. You have them or you are numb. Those are the options.

Realize if you turn off your emotions, you cannot feel happy and joyful and excited. There will not be laughter in your life and laughter is what changes circumstances. Being able to balance sadness and finding reasons to see something as funny is essential for healing.

We want to give you some more helpful techniques for dealing with a loss.

Seek your Source. Sit and spend time with your Source. If that is a religious Source like a God who has a book that you can read, sit and read that book. Find passages and stories that address your kinds of loss and what the examples in the book did to grieve and how they handled their emotional pain. If your Source is like Kim's and there isn't a set book, perhaps attempt automatic writing, channeling, or meditation in order to connect. It is essential to seek your Source first. (In Chapter 8, Kim will guide you to find a personal relationship with your Source and help you to connect. Don't hesitate to access those meditations. https://ditl-meditation.kimbeam.com/)

Sleep. Practice good sleep hygiene. Get to bed early. Make sleep a ritual, part of a nighttime routine. Close down your devices early. Play soft music if that's your thing. Find a good book to read - not an electronic book, a paper book. Screens keep your brain awake; paper books allow the brain to quiet down. Adjust lighting. There are some people who would say if sleep has been a problem, once nighttime hits, turn off all overhead lights, turn off all screens (TV, tablets, and phones), and only use candles to create quiet in the brain. That last bit might seem extreme, but if you are desperate for sleep, desperate times call for desperate measures. When Kim's dad died, she used a weighted blanket at night to help her sleep. It was 15 pounds and the right amount of weight to give her peace. Once she started using it, sleep came.

Kim just recently found mouth tape. Her biometric devices that studied her sleep showed the mouth tape gave her better deep sleep and better REM.

Journal. Write it out. Be real, authentic, and yourself in the pages. Don't worry about who will read it or how you sound. Allow your true self and your feelings the freedom to be themselves. Be unabashedly real about your experiences. Later if you go back and read it, put judgement aside and know this is a perfect screenshot of where you were emotionally at that time. It will be a barometer for how much you have grown. (Kim has been known to judge the self she finds in journals so harshly she is ashamed and throws them away so others can't read how "pathetic" - her word not ours - she is. We caution against this. There is so much to learn about your own growth and where you are when you wrote it to where you are when you go back and read it. So much growth to be celebrated.)

Therapy. Kim has been to both therapists and hypnotherapists. She has spent a lot of time in therapy. She finds it grounding and encouraging.

Your Great Cloud of Witnesses. We've already talked about these people quite a bit. But one of the things we want to say here, is when you are in pain, struggling, and taking time to heal, it's important to intentionally call them in and let them know what you need. Let them know you need their intentional support. Let them know you want to heal and then thank them for listening to the same stories over and over and over and over again.

Also, for some pain and grief, it's possible in this healing time, getting up and doing something is just not possible. Don't be afraid to ask them to come and clean your bathroom, bring a meal, or do something that you are just dreading doing. Your Great Cloud of Witnesses wants to be there for you. By asking them to do something you just can't face, you are actually honoring the friendship by saying, "Help."

(When Kim's best friend who now lives in Abu Dhabi gave birth to both of her children, about three weeks after the baby's arrival, Kim showed up in junky clothes and cleaned her bathroom both times, knowing that her friend and her spouse just didn't have it in them to get it done.)

Find things (activities, places, experiences, people) that light you up. When a wound opens, it's so easy to fill it up with business, activities, sounds, and noise, filling your life with parties and too many people. We encourage you to fill the wound with things that light you up. Try new things: maybe you take a pottery class, or ...here in

Philadelphia there is the School of Circus Arts, which has beginner classes. That last option might be harder than you think you can handle, which it would be for Kim. Kim cried when she went to the local gym for the first time and signed up with a trainer (and that was just seven months ago, as of this writing!). It was such a challenging and life changing move for her. Maybe you join a dance class. Maybe you start taking yourself out on solo dates, find new places to eat and have a small adventure along the way by going to a new area of your community or by finding new shops to explore.

Allowing time and space for your emotions while you are hurting is extremely important and running away from them is not going to help you heal. It's going to prolong your suffering.

Acknowledging how you feel when you feel that way, and letting yourself feel the contrast between what you want and what you don't have allows your body and your being to find more peace. Pay attention to the content of the material you take in (the TV shows, the books you read, the movies you watch, the content in your doomscroll). What you spend your time with also matters. Drowning yourself in other people's negative viewpoints will hinder your ability to heal. We want to explore in the next chapter how what you take in affects your mood, vibration, and being.

Chapter Six

What You Take In Matters

Kim lived with a man briefly for about a year and a half. When he moved in, he brought in his TV, and set up his office in her spare bedroom. She welcomed these things when he moved in.

When it was time for him to move out, he took his TV with him. He looked at her and said, "Are you getting a new TV?"

She said, "I wasn't planning on it."

He said, "How are we going to keep watching *Game of Thrones* together?"

She said, "Are you planning on buying me a TV?"

He scoffed.

To which Kim said, "Then we aren't watching *Game of Thrones* together."

After he moved out, Kim's father kept trying to buy her a TV.

She really didn't want to watch TV and didn't see a need for one. She didn't have time. She didn't want to use TV to numb herself. She was focused on other things and a TV was not important to her. She figured if she wanted to watch something, she could stream it. But let us be honest with you and out her a little, she hasn't streamed anything in probably two years - other than independent news content creators on YouTube and doom-scrolling.

She's been pretty much single since that boyfriend moved out in 2019. Sitting down on a Friday night to watch something together with someone isn't something she does. She goes out to dinner with her mom on Friday nights, then she goes grocery shopping.

Kim is aware of what is going on in the world and what the problems are, but she does not invite that rectangle of noise into her space at this time. She is aware that if she were to meet somebody, that somebody would likely really want a TV. We will add, she already has it in her head that he can put the TV in his man cave.

For years, since Kim was in her early twenties and teaching 7th graders, she has been using the expression, "Garbage in; garbage out."

She also says things like, "What you pay attention to grows," and "Whatever you feed yourself is what you get out."

Let us give an example. Kim started to read a book that was a modern retelling of *Peter Pan*. It was mostly told from Wendy and Captain Hook's perspective, making Captain Hook the protagonist. Only Captain Hook was truly evil and in the second or third chapter, the writer told a very well written, very descriptive account of a murder Captain Hook committed. The description was vivid and alluring. It was brilliantly told and alive on the page. Which also made it very graphic.

To be honest, by the time the murder occurred, Kim was kind of hooked (no pun intended) into the characters (and how despicable most of them were) and the plot. Only the murder scene was so well written, she found the gore of it to be too much for her now. She returned the book early, without getting much past that gory murder scene. But even now, she wonders how it turned out for Wendy, and Hook, and Peter whom Hook wanted to murder very much.

What surprised Kim was how disgusted and sickened it made her to watch an imaginary man suffer.

This has not been how she has felt in the past. *Game of Thrones'* violence didn't create this kind of visceral reaction.

So much of your TV and news has become sensational. So much of what is aired is aired to push the envelope. To create shock and awe. To keep people in fear in order to maintain ratings.

That is old world thinking.

It is limiting to think that fear is the only thing that sells.

Right now, the way we have done literature and story has been set in the idea there must be conflict for a story to unfold. Or if it's a Rom Com, the main characters need to stop talking to each other. These are tropes and they are old. There are new plots and stories coming. Soon the old stories and tropes will be boring and "dead" in that they will no longer feel alive and exciting. Soon, the new ways of writing and telling stories will include story telling that creates communities and conflict will no longer be a part of the trope. There are new plot ideas coming that will open the door to a couple coming together and growing together through the struggles and changes. The new exciting storyline will be how they stay together to grow stronger and more dynamic as a couple rather than breaking up when things get challenging.

This shift that is affecting stories overall will not just stop there. It will change the way people see the world. What will light people up will be stories of collaboration, stories where people work together to solve problems, stories where the hero is not just one person but many working together to create lasting change for the good of others. Instead of how the current rom-com trope runs, where the couple has to stop talking to create the tension, soon, love stories will show how being together makes the couple stronger.

During the Pandemic, Kim watched John Krakowski's *Good News Network* that he aired about eight episodes of on YouTube. In each episode, he highlighted the positive things going on in the world. She also started to read books that encouraged her to feel good. This is around when Kim's romance novel binge reading really took off. She read uncountable numbers of romance novels – sometimes up to three or four a week.

However, we are going to spill some beans here. In the last couple of days (in June and July of 2025), Kim has become bored of romance novels. She has no idea what to read, because she's tired of so many of the traditional plots of all stories. She is looking for the kind of book she wants to read, only that kind of book hasn't really been written yet.

To satisfy her craving for a book she wants to read, Kim has started to write a novel. One of the things we keep telling her is that we don't want conflict in this novel. She keeps asking, "How do you write a book without conflict?"

We keep telling her, "We will show you. There won't be conflict, but the reader will be driven to read."

To be honest, the lack of conflict is actually what will be exciting.

Humanity is tiring of the old ways of doing things. They are tired of the same scenarios that have happened over and over.

Humanity is tired of the "Us versus Them" story. That there must be a loser and winner. That one side triumphs over the other side. This is an old paradigm of thinking.

Kim thinks about this a lot. Do you know the quickest way to form a bond with someone? Talk trash about a third person. Instantly you have a shared connection and a shared secret.

Kim has never been one to stay here long though. Kim was friends with a girl in college, who met a man, got married over the summer, and didn't return to the college their Junior year. They transferred to a school in Philadelphia. Kim met a person who also knew that couple. The only connection this person and Kim shared was this couple and so they just talked bad about them together. Kim and this person talked about them so much that Kim began to sincerely wonder how her friend was doing. So, one day after a particularly terrible trash talking, Kim went back to her dorm room and called her friend. Kim sincerely cared and missed her. They had a long conversation and Kim went back to the college acquaintance on campus and said, "Look. They got married. They did it. Instead of talking bad about them and how we think it's a bad idea, we have to figure out ways to support them as they work through whatever this marriage is going to look like." To be honest, they are still married, like 30 years later. That person at the college? That person stopped talking to Kim. That person embraced his anger and judgement, and turned that anger and judgement on Kim for reaching out to her friend, and changing the story. Instead of being one of divisiveness, Kim turned it into peace, love, acceptance, and encouragement. That person on campus was not willing to go there.

But this is where all humanity is going. The old stories of someone must lose, or one person can have "it all," while somebody else has nothing? This is old thinking.

We want to help you understand and see. These old patterns keep you trapped. They hold you in a space that keeps you stuck. The belief that you don't measure up, that you are not enough, that you are too much, that you can't have it all, that you must choose between yes and something "less than"? That's not the future we want you to walk into.

The more you look at the world around you as portrayed by the media and the movies, the more you see the split between the Have and Have Not, the Special and the Not Special, the Wanting and the Having, or should we say instead, the Wanting and the Never Getting. The point we really want to stress here is to check the content of what you're filling your brain with. What you fill your brain with also trickles down to your heart and helps you create definitions and beliefs in this life that don't necessarily serve you. In fact these beliefs could, in fact, hurt you.

Self definitions that are created from a limited space will hinder you. Marketers use your desires and weaknesses against you intentionally to get you to buy their products.

Right now on planet Earth, there is a general belief about how things work. Please hear this – there is a shift coming that will make these old beliefs antiquated and boring. Kim is already experiencing this. She is tired of old stories of couples who stop talking to each other, of violence to keep attention, of cruelty to prove how evil someone is. Kim is interested in the kindness, the love, the connection, the feeling that anything is possible, the feelings of wonder, awe, excitement, and of good adventure.

We encourage you to find things that light you up, excite you, bring you joy, and help you grow into a soul that values love, kindness, goodness, and connection. You may already be a soul that values these things and so let this conversation encourage you to step away from other people's definitions of what is "good content." We encourage you to continue to enjoy content that lifts your soul and feeds your being. But notice if what used to make you feel lifted and fed no longer makes you feel that way. You are transforming and honoring that transformation is so important.

Finding content that lights you up isn't always easy.

We say the search for meaningful content is fulfilling because, in the end, you will find something that resonates with your heart's cry to be seen, encouraged, and lifted up by the content you take in.

It's okay if you stand alone in this and in the next chapter we want to talk about the power of listening to your Source, your Team even if it means you walk alone and have to walk away from everything you have known.

Chapter Seven

Why you Want to Walk with Your Source as Your Guidance

Years ago, Kim made the decision that she wanted to hear from Spirit, her Spiritual Team, if you will. At the time, she was in Christianity and was looking to hear from the Holy Spirit. She wanted to know God more.

Now she sees it as being connected, locked in, and aware. She hears it quickly when we say, "Yes," and when we say, "No." She is confident in her being able to hear those responses. She knows in her gut when something isn't going to go the way others think it's going to go. She is starting to get flashes of images and events - future or in alternate timelines. She is still learning and doesn't always know what to do with them.

For most of Kim's life, she has been asking to go deeper with us. We have been bringing people into Kim's life - over and over and over, who have been raising up Kim's vibration a little, by a little, by a little. It started in the church, bringing her to a church that would help train and hone her listening skills. We had her mentor under our beloved Steve. Then when that was becoming limiting, we moved her out of the church and had her study under Cristina Leeson, then Chris Duncan, then Heather Alice Shea. Kim was still hungry for more. So, we brought someone in to transform everything. We brought in Isabelle Zimmerman, an ascension teacher, to work with Kim for a total of 29 weeks consecutively - a total of six months. This meeting was not "a fluke thing." It was intentional. We wanted Kim in the pressure cooker of healing with Isabelle Zimmerman of Attracting Wisdom for a reason. Their work together helped both of them. Even with their sessions over, Kim makes Isabelle feel less alone and less like Isabelle is doing this work in a vacuum. Isabelle feels seen and supported by Kim, even though Kim was the client. Kim is so grateful for Isabelle, for Isabelle sees Kim for who she is, flaws, weaknesses, shortcomings, and humanness, and loves the stuffing out of her. Isabelle gives Kim unconditional positive regard, loving encouragement, and calls her ego out when Kim's ego is so mean and harsh on Kim.

Good spiritual teaching creates grounding and stability in a chaotic world.

Kim can feel and see the difference having an Ascension teacher has created.

Before working with Isabelle Zimmerman, we were actually talking to her all the time, but she couldn't always connect and hear us.

Please hear this – your Spiritual Team is talking to you all the time. Your antenna isn't up, or you have static like when a radio station starts to switch from one area to another, or it's like when you lose signal on a cell phone and you lose bars and it gets a little choppy and sometimes somebody sounds robotic and then they cut out completely. Your Team may not have any bars on your cell receptors inside your heart and brain. You have to consciously tell your Team that you want to create the reception bars inside your mind to hear your Team clearly. They don't come barging in – well, they do sometimes – but that's not the norm. Most of the time, you have to ask your Team to teach you how to hear them.

Isabelle Zimmerman starts her sessions with this phrase, "I wish to connect with my heart's energy." She does this because your heart's energy is connected to your Spiritual Team, your highest self, and your own inner wisdom. Your heart's energy runs through this lifetime, past lifetimes, or rather concurrent lifetimes. It helps you find your center and your purpose.

Once you are connected to your heart's energy, you can ask your Team for support. Your Team wants you to know that you are seen, loved, and supported.

Some people ask for signs. They name something very specific, just so their Team can show them They are paying attention and love them. Some people think that every time they see a dragonfly, a butterfly, a cardinal, or their animal of preference, it means that their Team is encouraging them.

We have a cautionary tale here though. Let's say you are asking for something like a job, a life partner, or a very specific thing like a specific house you want to buy. We want to stress in the best way possible that if you are asking for a sign while you're simultaneously asking for that thing we just listed, if you see that sign, it does not automatically mean you're going to get the thing for which you are asking. We want this to be so clear. The disappointment you can experience can be devastating. If you ask for something specific and then you ask for a sign, and every time you ask for the sign, your Team gives you the gift of a fulfilled sign, your lovely brain may associate that sign with a promise to give you the thing you want. Which in turn, can give comfort. Well, if that thing you are asking for doesn't come in, this can cause massive disappointment. It may cause you to stop asking for signs. It may stop you from communicating with your Spiritual Team, with your Source, altogether.

Kim asked for a sign when she really wanted a job. (This story is given in more detail in *Walk in Courage: Trusting the Whispers of Your Intuition.*) We gave her a sign repeatedly over and over to show her that we were with her. She saw the signs as proof she was going to get the job. When she didn't get the job she wanted, she thought the signs were lying to her.

The truth that she didn't see was we were showing her, over and over, we were with her. It didn't matter to us, so much, if she got the job. We wanted her to learn to trust us, to see us, and to know we were in her corner.

She saw the signs and interpreted it to mean she was getting the job. That was not completely what we had intended. We intended for her to trust us. She took the signs as proof of her getting the job. When the job wasn't offered to her, it caused her significant disappointment. She was deeply hurt that she didn't get the job and as a result of the entire experience she stopped asking for signs.

What we love about this moment is Kim has never seen this moment from our perspective. She has never known that we were using the signs to show her we saw her and were encouraging her. She took the signs as things she shouldn't trust. Now, she sees that the signs were given in love.

We want to encourage you to ask for signs to see that your Source is with you, but do not hold onto an outcome. Just because a sign comes, it doesn't mean your Source is bringing in the thing you want, in the way you want it. Let go of the outcomes. Let go of the way, the how, and the avenue of the thing you want coming in. Just let it be. Your Source hears and knows what you want. Allow your Source to respond to your requests in your Source's perfect way.

In the meantime, don't be afraid to ask for signs to be encouraged and to see that your Source loves you and is with you.

Your Source has plans for you, as we talked about at the beginning of this book. Your Source needs you to trust them. Not trusting your Spiritual Team to take care of you is like going out on an ocean in a boat without a guidance system. You are completely lost at sea. Even in the 1500s and 1600s, sailors had a guidance system which included an astrolabe and the stars. Starting a conversation with your Team is the most essential thing you can do to help you find peace and follow your purpose in this lifetime.

We've already addressed how your emotions are part of your guidance system. You can sense when something is good or bad based on your emotional reaction to it. This is also a part of your Spiritual Team's conversation with you. If you don't have peace, you aren't going in the right direction.

Peace is annoying in that you have to learn how peace works in your body. You have to know where it sits and how it lands. You also have to learn what it feels like when you don't have peace, how you react and act when peace is absent.

Honestly, peace is experiential.

Let's be honest. Most of this life is experiential. You are having a human experience and if nobody taught you the importance of connecting to your Spiritual Team, and the importance of listening to your emotions, some of this may feel foolish and silly.

As a human in society today, you came from a long line of historians, who put more emphasis on science, logic, reasoning, and the ego, rather than using your Spiritual Team and your feelings to solve your problems. But we are saying if you want to be sure that you are headed in the direction that is best for your growth, and finding and fulfilling your purpose in this lifetime, connecting to your inner self, connecting to your Spiritual Team, and connecting to your emotions are essential. Happiness and contentment in life come when you know that what you are doing lines up with the goals you created before you got here. If there is a feeling of disconnect inside of you, a feeling that what you spend the majority of your day doing is not a part of what fulfills you, then you know what you are doing is not a part of your soul purpose. Finding the things that light you up is essential in order to create fulfillment of the goals that you came here to fulfill.

Connecting with your Team is essential. Even if you found your soul purpose and you're doing things that light you up, even if you are excited about what you are doing here, your Spiritual Team has another move for you. There is always more to learn, more to experience, more to accomplish, more ways to level up. There's always more to be done. Your Source wants you to continue to learn and grow. You aren't meant to stay stagnant. Stagnant waters fester. They create bugs. They also cause overgrowth and then stop being water. They become marsh and then eventually land. Which is all dried up and no longer water. You need to be a flowing body of water to make sure that you are in the stream of growth. Life is happening for you, for your maximum potential of experiences and growth. Connecting with your Spiritual Team is critical in fulfilling all that you can possibly fulfill in this lifetime.

Let us talk to you about how to connect with your Spiritual Team on an even deeper level in the next chapter.

Chapter Eight

How to Connect with Your Source

https://ditl-meditation.kimbeam.com/

We recorded three meditations for you to experience how to talk to a Guide. We know we used the word Guide and, hopefully, that is not a turn off or deterrent to you. We also hope that there is enough of an introduction in the beginning of each audio recording that gets you into your ability to see and hear in the meditation. We want you to play. We want your inner child to have fun. We hope you allow your ego and your logic to fall away and that you allow yourself to play a little with the recordings.

It may take a number of listens to get you into the right headspace. One recording may be better than another recording. You may find that you like number two better than you like number one or you like number three best out of all of them, which is perfect. That is why there are three of them.

Each one is slightly different. There's an animal in each one. Take a mental note of the animal that shows up and then, after the listen, maybe Google or research the spiritual meaning of that animal. Notice the colors we ask you to notice - if the animal had an unusual eye color or if the animal was an unusual color itself – like if you see a purple bear. Maybe you want to look up the spiritual meaning of that color as well. In the experience for number three, there is a bookcase. Maybe you saw a specific title of a book on that bookcase. Take note of the book that you saw. Also in experience number three, we ask you to drop an object and pick up an object. Notice what those objects are.

Kim once led one of these online and one of the attendants said he dropped his car keys on the table, leaving them behind. He was also listening to the meditation while stranded in a town in the middle of a long travel because his car was broken down. Most of the time, keys mean you have hit a higher level in your spiritual growth; you've opened new doors. In this case, we told Kim it was him dropping his feelings and attachment to the car, the frustration, and the feeling of being trapped. So the meanings can be different given your circumstances.

When Kim was recording the number three experience, she was envisioning the meditation while she was recording it. There's a kitchen in the meditation. For Kim, when she moved into that meditation kitchen, there was something cooking at that time. Kim had her childhood favorite dish pop through her mind, complete with how the dish made her feel, how it smelled, and how it tasted. Since Kim is now dairy-free, gluten-free, and sugar-free there is no way Kim will ever eat this dish again. However it was the dish that was cooking when she walked in the kitchen in this experience. We helped this memory come alive for her because we love her.

The most important part of each of the meditations is the actual conversation with your Spiritual Team Member - your guide.

Use the QR Code or this link: https://ditl-meditation.kimbeam.com/ to find the recordings, then come back here when you are done. You may want to have a journal by your side so that you can take notes as soon as you come out of the experience.

You may have bumped into an angel. You may have bumped into an alien. You may have bumped into an ancestor. How did you react when you saw them? Was it peaceful or was it emotionally overwhelming? Did you feel loved, accepted, appreciated, or encouraged?

Then there's the conversation. What happened in that conversation? What was said? How did this conversation make you feel? Were there words or phrases you absolutely wanted to remember?

Now that you've had a conversation with your Source, your Guide, whatever word you want to use, what do you do with this information?

First, we recommend that you journal or you find a way to hold onto the words. Whether that's on the notes app in your phone, on a Google doc, or actually hand written in a paper journal. The method is completely up to you.

We also ask if there is something specific that your Guide wanted you to know? We ask that those words get special focus. Especially write those words down because it's very likely you will forget them. Maybe you put it on an index card and stick them to your fridge; or maybe you write them on a Post-It note and you stick them to the bathroom mirror; or maybe you put them on a Post-It note and you put them in your car, so you see it while you're getting in and out along your travels; or maybe you put it by your office desk, because you sit there so much during the day.

We want those words to resonate deeply. We want those words to become internalized and truth giving. We want them to become so much a part of your being that you know them to be your truth deep in your core. This is one of the ways you change from the inside out.

Words get dismissed so easily. Especially kind words. These are words that you need to hear. This is the encouragement that you have been looking for. We encourage you to hold on to this experience and we encourage you to find ways to give these words a priority in your life.

Use these recordings over and over and over again, as needed to help you find your direction, your Source, your purpose, and encouragement along the way.

Your Guides, your Source, and your Spiritual Team want to be a part of your daily life. They want to be an active player in the game that is your experience. They want you to know that you are valued and treasured, and that they are so incredibly proud of you. They love you. They just really appreciate all of the work that you are doing. The more that you can connect with them, the more that you will feel that acceptance, appreciation, encouragement, and delight.

We have some house keeping things we want to put here at the end of this chapter.

We know we used the word Guides in the recordings and if that is a stumbling block for you, we apologize. We wanted to be sure we were meeting only one member of your Spiritual Team. Your Spiritual Team is made of components and we chose the word "Guide" for only one of the components of that Team.

Also, if in the unlikely event that your Guide said something that wasn't helpful to you and maybe those words were actually painful, so many things to say! It wasn't a Guide. It wasn't a true experience, and please forget whatever happened in that meditation immediately. That's not how your Guides work and negative words are not from your Team. We would recommend that you try the mediation over, looking to seek your highest and best self for wisdom and understanding.

If, as you were doing the meditation, you got "popped out" or you didn't see anything, we would recommend you using one of the meditations daily until your ego allows you to drop fear and experience fun.

This is not a chapter to skip. In fact, this might be the most important chapter in the book. These meditations are here for you to come back to over, and over, and over again. We don't want you to miss the good that is in the experience. A lot of what happens during spiritual growth is experiential. It's moving away from what you know with your head and moving into the unseen realms. That is done energetically. That is done spiritually. It is a practice.

Let these meditations, other meditations, or just your own silent meditations be a guiding light for you.

Please know, what happens inside the meditation space is real. It is real.

We ask that if you haven't actually done the meditations that you pause and do them. Give your Spiritual Team an opportunity to meet with you, connect with you, encourage you, and show you love. They really do think you are doing a fantastic job! When you hear those words from your Source directly, they have so much more power and lasting effect. Besides, they know you better than we do. They've been with you from the start and they will be with you in the end.

Kim is always so curious as to how people are receiving such things. After you do the meditation practices, if you want to send her an email she would love to read it and hear about your experiences. She would love to hear how this landed for you. Please, don't be shy. Reach out and tell her what happened for you in the meditation experiences using info@kimbeam.com. We are sincerely thrilled about your opportunities to connect with your Team so that you can dive even deeper into your purpose.

Your Team is also there to support you when things get hard. That is something we want to explore in the next chapter.

Chapter Nine

How to Manage When Your Team Asks You To Do Uncomfortable Things

There are times when you are comfortable and you know what you're doing. You think you are set in your job, in your life. Then Source comes in and shakes things up.

Now that you've gone through Chapter 8: How to Connect with Your Source, you know a little about how your Source talks to you, and how they connect with you. Now that a connection is established, you can hear them. Now that you know how they present themselves to you, you will be more open and aware of your Spiritual Team and what they are telling you, or maybe even asking of you.

As you grow in your knowledge of your Source, they may ask you to do things that just don't feel natural or normal. They may actually ask you to do things that don't make sense. They may ask you to move or to leave a job you really like. They may even ask you to break up with the person you are committed to. These are not easy circumstances, but there are reasons why they ask you to do hard things.

Kim was living with the man she mentioned before – the one with the TV. He and Kim were living together for a little while, and she was exploring a whole bunch of different alternative therapies, from aromatherapy to Mindfulness-Based Stress Reduction (MBSR). When MBSR led her to meditation and seven day silent retreats, her Team told her to start listening to her intuition. She found a psychic, who also taught people how to tap into their intuition. In one of her meetings with this woman, the woman told her to break up with her boyfriend. She didn't just say, "Break up with him," but she gave reasons that Kim couldn't argue with. She said that Kim's boyfriend was taking money from her; and that her boyfriend was making Kim's life harder, rather than helping. He was blocking her growth and was inhibiting her ability to become who her Source wanted her to be. It took Kim about two months after that meeting to finally end the relationship, and the boyfriend made the joke, not really a joke, that they survived all her other things: aromatherapy, and knitting, but they couldn't survive her studying meditation.

The thing with meditation is that it gets you quiet and it allows you to really hear yourself, your voice, your own ego, and your Team. It allows you to get in touch with your spiritual side. Meditation allows you the opportunity to explore both your humanity and your spirituality.

When you get quiet with your Team and there is something they need to address, it can get uncomfortable. They will show you something and you will see it. Not only will you see it, but you will feel it and you will know it. But, sometimes you don't *really* want to see it, right? Like you see it and you hear it, but then you dismiss it or you push it away. Maybe it's just too uncomfortable. Or maybe right then, you want to be in your own little bubble.

The thing is, your Source is asking for you to level up. All the time. Step up into bigger and bolder. More brave actions and more responsibility. Doing things that level up your vibration and level up your experiences in this lifetime.

There was a moment in Kim's life when she was hanging out with a man who had a really good job. However, he was being given the opportunity for promotion in a different corporation. There was a part of him that was married to the corporation he was already working for. He believed in his current corporation's vision. He believed in the family atmosphere the corporation he worked for created. He believed in the work he was doing and he had already had some major successes with that organization. However, he was being wooed by a much more prestigious organization, one that was making an even more important and positive impact on all of humanity. (That seems a bold statement, but trust us, it's true.) Kim met with this man in his office one day as he was wrestling with his decision to stay where he was or to go to this bigger opportunity.

Kim said, "I basically have one thing to say to you." She knew the things she was about to say came from her Source, and so she boldly said, "Don't let the successes of your past stop you from having bigger successes in the future. Don't let your love for what you have created in this organization stop you from creating even bigger successes in another organization. Don't let the you holding onto the past stop you from the 'amazing' you are supposed to create in your future."

He responded with, "That was really well said."

He did wind up accepting the new position in the new corporation.

As he was packing up his office, Kim visited with him and said, "I didn't know if you were going to take the job."

He replied, "Honestly, I didn't know if I was going to take it either."

Sometimes your Team is trying to get you to move and you don't want to be moved. Sometimes opportunities open before you and you let them pass you by because it's not what you want at this moment. Maybe you feel you're not ready. Maybe you have an excuse, or five.

Whatever is your reason that you let the opportunity go, your Source will not let you stay stuck. If they really want you to move, they will move you. You can either move when it feels like your decision to move (which is way more comfortable) or they will move you when it is really against your will (which is super uncomfortable).

There is a plan. There is an ultimate goal and that ultimate goal is tied to the purpose of your lifetime. If something feels unfair or feels difficult, it may be because you weren't willing to move when you were first given direction to move. Your Team is always working for your highest good. They are always working out of love and appreciation for you. They know your goals and your purposes in this lifetime. They will protect you from derailing yourself from that purpose and those goals. This is where discomfort can arise. Because what you think you want in your humanity is not what you want in your spirituality. Your soul purpose and your human purpose can sometimes be at odds.

Kim likes to say, "When your head and your heart are not in line with each other it causes problems." It can cause anxiety. It can cause depression. It can cause other mental health concerns. It can cause physical concerns - serious medical conditions that need medical intervention.

When your head and your heart are not in line with each other there is a kind of war going on inside your body. Your head and your ego want one thing and your heart wants something else. When you are tapped into your Source and they ask you to do big things, our suggestion is to sit and breathe with those requests. Take them to your ...we'll say meditation space. But whatever is that space for you — a space where you create openness, a conversation, an opportunity for dialogue between you and your Spiritual Team. A conversation between you, your Source, and your ego. All three come together to have a conversation about the thing you are being asked to do by your Spiritual Team, especially if that request is overwhelming and difficult.

The truth is you are asked to do overwhelming and difficult things.

Your Spiritual Team will give you the strength to do what needs to be done. They will show up. They will show you how. They will motivate you to accomplish the task. They will guide you through every step of the journey. They will support you. They will not leave you alone. They will be with you every step of the way, as you step forward into the scary that they are asking you to accomplish.

We will also say if you do not choose to step forward into the scary that they are asking you to accomplish, they might move you anyway. Without your consent. When you don't consent, it tends to be more dramatic and possibly traumatic. Let us explain, because this sounds threatening or menacing and we don't mean it that way. Let's say your Spiritual Team asks you to leave your job and you don't. They give you multiple opportunities to leave your job and you don't take any of them. Knowing what is best for you, your Spiritual Team will have the job leave you. You will get fired or let go. Some other circumstance will occur. Because you weren't willing to move, they made the move for you. In that moment, it might not feel like that was for your good. In fact, there were probably all sorts of negative emotions around it. But if you had left when they first asked you to, the negative feelings wouldn't have been there at all.

In another scenario, say they ask you to separate from your spouse and you don't. They give you opportunity after opportunity to make the break yourself. They show you places to live that really light you up, but still you choose to ignore the instructions to leave your spouse. They may even give you a job opportunity separated from your spouse, but you ignore it. They might even show you reason after reason after reason why it's better for you and your spouse to separate, like Kim saw with the TV boyfriend. But still, you don't separate. It will then be orchestrated that your spouse will leave you.

For Kim, cancer was the one thing she told her Source she wasn't doing. She said to us when she was being diagnosed, "I don't have cancer. I'm not doing chemo. It's not happening." But then it did. Because it did, because she had chemotherapy for Hodgkin's, she's writing this book for you now. Because of the diagnosis, treatment, and all that she experienced in those moments and after, she transformed into the woman she is today, dancing in the light and giving you a guide for your own awakening.

(Now for the human that didn't see the negative things coming -- if, Dear Reader, you didn't see being let go from your job or you didn't see your spouse leaving -- to you we want to say, you are being given an opportunity to learn and grow. Yes, there is pain; we are not belittling that pain. We aren't minimizing it either. We are also saying that this is an opportunity for learning and growth if you allow it to be such. There is much more ahead of you that this loss is training you for, preparing you for. Trust your Spiritual Team. When you are ready, sit with your Source, and allow your Source to talk to you and show you how this is changing your life for the good and will one day create happiness if you let it. That day is not today. Today might be a day for bringing your tears, anger, and pain to your Spiritual Team.)

Many humans lose their minds, their faith, and their trust when such negative things occur. They blame the universe. They blame other people. They blame their Source. Rarely do they blame themselves. Ultimately if you are tapped into your Source and you are hearing them and you are looking to learn and grow and change and transform, they will give you grace and encouragement as you work toward your mutual goals.

This is what we want you to hear: ultimately your Team's goals are your goals. Your Team's goals will bring in growth, change, joy, and happiness. It's not bad when they ask you to do big and hard things. In fact, it is actually an honor, because they know you can handle the request. You may not feel like you can handle the request, but they are with you every step of the way. Just ask them and they will show you.

Ultimately, any request that they give is for your highest good. When an uncomfortable request comes in: one, be honored you've made it to a point where they can ask for something challenging; two, be excited you heard it in the first place; and, three, know that they will give you the resources and the wherewithal to accomplish what may feel to be an impossible task. For them, this is not impossible.

They would not ask it of you if ultimately there weren't a higher purpose.

This is a chance for you to walk in trust and know that you are leveling up.

For them, this is a chance for them to show you what a life of adventure following Source can be.

Chapter Ten

Putting It All Together

Dear Reader, we are so excited that you made it this far in this book! We are so excited that you have come to sit with us, spend time with us, hear our stories, and hear our message to you. We are so happy that you are exploring your spiritual side and what awakening feels like. We are so excited to be able to share with you that you are not going nutty and that you are absolutely normal. You are just awakening to another realm.

You are seeing the world in a new way.

We are very happy you are here!

Does this mean that you might lose some friendships? Yes.

Does this mean that you might have a bit of heartache? Yes.

Does this mean that you are feeling a bit alone in this world? Yes.

More importantly than all of that, awakening to your Spiritual Team is the most important thing you can do.

Your Spiritual Team has guidance for you and insight to help ensure that you are on the path that's right for you. They help you create a better life. They awaken your heart to the more you have been craving and help you to find that you are actually not alone in this universe, on this planet, at this time. You are seen, understood, and held.

Your Spiritual Team has amazing support for you. They have the perfect people to bring into your life if you are willing to see them. If you are willing to change your vibration, they have amazing gifts waiting for you. However, until you raise your vibration, you aren't at a place where you're able to accept all that your Spiritual Team has to give to you in this lifetime.

By acknowledging that you are a spirit having a human experience, you are saying to your Spiritual Team, "I want everything that this life and this world has for me."

You will then work to raise your vibration by getting to know your Spiritual Team (one Guide at a time) and knowing in your core that the experiences you are having in this life are the ones you are supposed to be having. If you are having them, they are the ones that are meant to happen. This life is not a collage of accidents. There is not just one path in the life you are living. There are multiple paths and sometimes they lead to the same spiritual goals, the same learning points. Sometimes, you get to choose the path for yourself. Sometimes, they practically force you down the path you are supposed to be walking.

You are in co-creation with your Spiritual Team. They have a plan and you have a plan. The two of you are coming together to work it out as one. It may look a little sloppy at first, as you intentionally work to co-create with your Team. It may look like you don't know what you're doing. (Let's be honest, who really does know what they are doing? Kim feels lost most of the time. Then she looks up at us and asks, "Is this right?" and we just say, "Yup! Keep moving forward!") For you, it might feel a little bit like you're making mistakes or that you are misinterpreting.

Let's be honest. You probably are misinterpreting. That happens a lot until humans learn how their Team talks to them. Do you know how many times Kim has stopped listening to Source because she thought she was getting it wrong? But every time she shut us down, she came back to us. Why? Because she knew that trying to hear us was better than trying to figure it out on her own.

It's okay. It's okay. It's okay.
It's okay to mess up.
It's all okay.
Peace.

What really matters is that you try and that you continue to work on hearing your Team, that you give them opportunities to speak, that you give them opportunities to show you that they love you. What really matters is that you give your Spiritual Team opportunities to show you that they are with you. It also really matters that your Spiritual Team wants what is best for you. Your Source is your biggest support and your biggest cheerleaders. Your Source loves you unconditionally.

We don't know if you really heard that so we will say it again.

Your Spiritual Team loves you unconditionally.

As much as you might hate this, the truth is, your Spiritual Team knows what's best for you. We know that's such a challenging thing to hear, because you think you know what's best for you. Your ego doesn't like this very much at all.

But let's have an honest conversation about your ego.

How many times has your ego (that loud know-it-all voice in your head) gotten you into trouble and then said it was your fault that you weren't listening to your intuition enough? Or how many times has your ego told you that you weren't listening to your Spiritual Team, your friends, your gut, your family enough?

Your ego never takes responsibility, but takes all of the credit.

For once, allow your Spiritual Team to be in balance with your ego or maybe even put your Spiritual Team in the driver's seat and shove your ego in the trunk. It's loud. It's obnoxious. Your ego makes a lot of noise and it tells you, "You're wrong." It insults you all the time.

Your Spiritual Team will never, ever, ever make you feel bad about yourself. They love you unconditionally. Your Spiritual Team is so excited that you are awakening. Your Spiritual Team is so excited you are learning how to seek them, and how to find them.

Does that mean your life might get a little bumpy to start, or even in the middle? The answer is yes, it's likely to be bumpy. Let's be honest. Your life is going to get bumpy anyway. You might as well get bumpy with your Spiritual Team's support rather than bumpy without their support.

You came to Earth in this lifetime, in this incarnation, in this body, to have experiences, to learn and grow and to fulfill your purpose. That is why you are here. Your Spiritual Team is on your side to help you fulfill all of those goals. The more you learn how to listen and trust and know them, the more you will be able to walk in all of the magnificence that this lifetime has for you. Sitting and listening to your Team, learning how they speak to you, finding ways to connect with them are essential skills in order to achieve overall contentment and purpose.

We hope that this book has helped you just a little bit down that path of knowing you are being seen and supported by Source. We also hope you have grown in the knowledge that you can ultimately trust your Source. Your Source's only job is to help you fulfill that which you have set out to fulfill in this lifetime.

We are so proud of you and we love you so much. We thank you for letting us speak into your life at this time.

May you find the peace and the fulfillment for which you are looking.

What Happens Now?!

Please leave a review!

If this book has touched your heart or sparked a change in your life, I'd be deeply grateful if you could take a moment to share your experience. Your feedback helps others discover the insights and inspiration within these pages, and it supports me in continuing to share my journey and wisdom with the world. Head over to Amazon or wherever you purchased this book, and leave an honest review. Your words truly make a difference and help others on their path to self-discovery and empowerment.

Feel like you want a one-on-one reading with me?

There are a few ways that we can connect for you to get a live reading with me.

If you are okay with a public reading and having people hear the words I have for you, there are a few options:

While I am still in the growing phase of my journey, I have been opening my Zoom room at least once a month for two hours. Anyone who signs up for VIP is guaranteed a reading. But you can just pop in for free and I will try to get to as many people in the room as possible. The great thing about being in the room is that when I give words to someone, they can be words for you too. There is a power and an energy in just being present.

When I am "big," I will stop doing Zoom rooms and move to Live Events. There you will have an opportunity to write a question on a card for me and I will maybe answer it from the stage. Or, I might answer it on my podcast, *Intuitive Insights with Kim Beam.*

Then there's the podcast. It's a chance for people to meet with me in a private Zoom room for free and have a live 15 minute reading with me. I record these and put them out as an audio podcast, on YouTube, and as reels.

You can sign up for the Zoom Room and Podcasts on my webpage: www.kimbeam.com. Live event information will also be on my website.

If you are not okay with a live reading where others are listening in:

On my website, www.kimbeam.com, there is a page to sign up for private readings with me.

But my other *FAVORITE* way to connect is through email!

Sure, I jones for Live Events where we are all together and I can give healing and readings right there in person. *That's my jam.* But Live Events aren't every day. My emails are three times a week and a chance for you to hear right from me. My emails are not your normal marketing emails. Sure, at the bottom of them I tell you what's coming up, like Zoom Rooms, Live Events, book releases, and other such things. But my emails? They are wacky and wonderful and weird and delightful. You *must* read them. They come out three times a week and the commitment is not a large one. Sign up at www.kimbeam.com to get on the newsletter listy. Then you will read about my daily thoughts, or on Fridays I send a channeled message. You really don't want to miss out on them!

Other ways to connect with me:

Follow me on the socials: @IamKimBeam on Instagram, Facebook, TikTok, and Substack. I am also on YouTube (@IamKimBeam2) and LinkedIn (https://www.linkedin.com/in/kimberly-beam-5575144/).

Thank you so much for your support and for being a part of this journey. I would love to meet with you and have you become a member of my community. So, reach out and I will be in touch with ways we can connect in Zoom Rooms, Live Events, and in my rambly words in an email.

Big Love!

Kim

About the Author

Kim Beam supports people in their individual circumstances, listening to her Spiritual Team for insight and encouragement. At her live events, Kim gives attendees opportunities to ask their burning questions, then engages with them as she taps into Source for responses, and offers healing.

With over 20 years of experience in developing her intuition and providing intuitive readings, Kim has transitioned from a passionate novice to a recognized expert. Her work has garnered acclaim. She is now a #1 Amazon Best-Selling Author for her book _Walk in Courage: Trusting the Whispers of Your Intuition_. She has been featured at the Emmy Gifting Suite 2024, in Real Simple (September 2024), Success Savvy Magazine (October 2024), Medium (November 2022, January 2023), CanvasRebel (August 2023), Vitality Digest (October 2024), Insight Timer, and on NBC and WSFL. Kim Beam has an upcoming appearance in Season 2 of _Recipe for Wellness_ airing on PBS with host Sanjay Raja.

Kim Beam holds Master's degrees in Social Work and Fine Arts, specializing in Creative Writing. With 12 years as a certified educator and over 10 years as a social worker, she is passionate and empathetic, dedicated to helping others find solutions to difficult problems. She sees what others overlook and shares insights that make people feel seen, heard, and supported on their journey.

Connect with Kim on social media at @IAmKimBeam on Facebook, Instagram, TikTok and Substack. Listen to her podcast *Intuitive Insights with Kim Beam* - where she offers free intuitive readings. Kim is currently hosting open readings in her Zoom room once or twice a month. Kim also hosts live events where she offers healing energy and channeled responses to people's individual questions. To learn more, visit her at KimBeam.com or reach out at Info@KimBeam.com.

Other Books by Kim Beam

Walk in Courage: Trusting the Wisdom of Your Intuition

What the Doctors Don't Tell You: One Woman's Journey Through Hodgkin's Lymphoma published under Kimberly Joy Beam